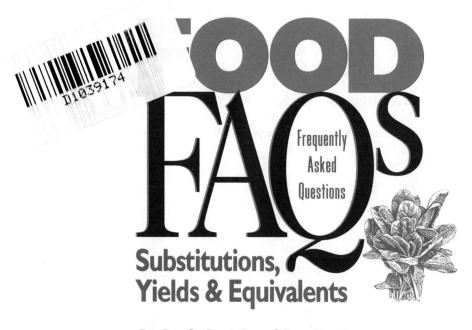

FOOD FAQS

Frequently Asked Questions

Substitutions, Yields & Equivalents

By Linda Resnik and Dee Brock

Published by FAQs Press, Tyler, Texas

Food FAQs: Substitutions, Yields & Equivalents

Copyright © 2000 by Linda Resnik

All rights reserved. No part of this book, including the interior design, cover design and page format, may be reproduced or transmitted in any form, by any means (electronic, photocopying, recording or otherwise) without the prior written permission of the copyright holder.

Published by FAQs Press, P.O. Box 130115, Tyler, Texas 75713 (903) 534-6587

First printing 2000

Library of Congress Catalog Card Number: 98-93812
ISBN 0-9667179-0-2

Food FAQs: Substitutions, Yields & Equivalents is available at special discounts for non-profit groups which select this book as a fund-raising product. Please contact the publisher for details.

Limits of Liability/Disclaimer of Warranty: The authors of this book have used their best efforts in preparing the book. The authors make no representation or warranties with respect to the accuracy or completeness of the contents of this book and specifically disclaim any implied warranties and shall in no event be liable for any loss of profit or any other commercial damage, including but not limited to special, incidental, consequential or other damages, as a result of the use of this book.

Book design and cover design by Carla Badaracco Design/Silver Spring, Maryland

Printed in the United States of America
10   9   8   7   6   5   4   3

Introduction

Welcome to *Food FAQs: Substitutions, Yields & Equivalents*, the first in a series of books designed to make every kitchen a little more efficient, every meal a little less frustrating and every cook a little happier.

Just how much of a particular ingredient do you need to meet your recipe's demands without either running short or having a lot left over? What can you substitute for an ingredient you don't have? Those are just the kinds of questions this book will help you answer.

Have you ever chopped onions until the tears ran down your face only to find you had prepared twice as much as the recipe required? You could have suffered less and wasted less had you known in advance approximately how much chopped onion results from an ounce of whole onion! Were you surprised (and maybe embarrassed) when the bunch of spinach you purchased yielded only half the amount you needed once you had trimmed and cooked it? Has the discovery that someone has already drunk all the tomato juice or eaten the last of the cream cheese ever left you stranded in the midst of preparing a recipe? Or in planning your menus, have you run across recipes that specify ingredients that you just know you cannot get in your local grocery store? If you are like most cooks, you can answer "yes" to each of those questions and many others like them. Certainly, that was true for us.

INTRODUCTION

Being compulsive fact-finders, we set out to find a kitchen reference book to help us out. Instead, we found bits and pieces of information in hundreds of books. But our quest to find a single, easy-to-use volume with comprehensive coverage of substitutions, yields and equivalents failed. So we decided to produce the book ourselves.

Now, after years of researching, testing, weighing, chopping, puréeing and measuring, we've compiled this handy volume with hundreds of substitutions, yields and equivalents that can help you buy exactly what you need and make-do with what you already have.

Designed for both novice and seasoned cooks, this ready reference does not include every possible food item. But it does cover those that are most widely available throughout the country and most likely to appear in contemporary recipes, as well as a number of specialty foods and exotic selections.

Getting the Most from *Food FAQs: Substitutions, Yields & Equivalents*

Food FAQs: Substitutions, Yields & Equivalents is divided into two major content sections: Substitutions (what you can use when you don't have an item specified) and Yields & Equivalents (how much you should buy or prepare to achieve certain measures). Within these sections, a number of **Food FAQs Quick Answers** offer general guidance or special instructions for broad categories of food. You will also find a full Index with hundreds of cross references at the back of the book.

Substitutions: In the **Substitutions** section, we've provided an alphabetical list of hundreds of common and not-so-common food items for which we have found one or more acceptable substitutes in cooking.

This section is not a "meal planning guide." When we note that you can substitute golden nugget squash for acorn squash, we're suggesting a reasonable replacement for an ingredient called for in a recipe, not an alternative dish. If you're planning a meal and want a change from the squash dish you usually prepare, consult your imagination, your best judgment or your favorite cookbook for that guidance!

Whenever you use substitutes in recipes, keep in mind that the results will not be identical to those achieved with the original ingredient. Some changes in taste – and maybe texture – are inevitable. But if you choose from among the substitutions in this book, you'll know that you have found a tested, successful alternative.

Some of the substitutions listed in this book can also help you modify your favorite recipes to lower-fat versions. Look throughout the section for the phrase *lower-fat alternative* to find these options.

Yields & Equivalents: Subdivided into common food categories, this section helps you plan ahead by noting how much of a particular ingredient you need to buy or use to equal a specified amount of a food item prepared in a specified way. In some cases, the information is as simple as telling you the equivalent measure in cups of ingredients that are purchased by weight in cans (such as chicken broth) or packages (such as dried fruits). In most cases, however, you will find the kinds of ingredients that are generally bought by the pound or the bunch, but are almost always called for in recipes in a trimmed, cut-up form measured by the cup or as a cooked ingredient. How many stalks of celery do you need to get ½ cup of thinly sliced celery? How many lemons do you need in order to get a ¼ cup of lemon juice? How many ounces or pounds of barley are needed for 3 cups of cooked barley?

The "Before Preparation" column in this section generally describes the most common variety or varieties of the item in the form most commonly available – for fruits and vegetables, this is usually a single item or a bunch, often with roots, pits or heavy stalks that will be trimmed away before using. For the most part, we've only included the fresh form of those items that are also available canned or frozen or processed.

The "After Preparation" column shows how much a specified amount of an item will yield once you have chopped, sliced, puréed or otherwise prepared it for use in a recipe. Of course, we trimmed the items to the parts normally eaten before we prepared and measured them. So, for something like a bunch of fresh spinach, which usually includes both leaves and stems when purchased, the notation in the "After Preparation" column refers to just the leaves, unless otherwise noted.

While we have gone to great lengths to provide you with accurate measurements, your results in food preparation will depend in part on how small you cut your pieces, whether you chop by hand or use a food processor, how tightly you pack them in a measuring cup and how moist the ingredients are. So, use these measurements as a guide and remember that all of the weights and volumes are approximate and should be treated as guides for your meal preparations.

Index: All food items featured in this book are listed alphabetically in the **Index**, along with the page(s) on which they can be found. Specific information about some foods is found within broader food categories, such as cheese, mushrooms and squash. But comprehensive cross-referencing will still let you find what you need, even if you don't remember that Gorgonzola is a cheese or that soba is a noodle.

We hope *Food FAQs: Substitutions, Yields & Equivalents* will do for you what it continues to do for us — make you more proficient in your kitchen and more organized on your grocery shopping forays. Whether it's a regular day to cook or a "rush rush" day when there's no time for either experimentation or an extra trip to the store, just look to this book as your best friend in the kitchen!

Substitutions

Ingredient Specified	Amount	Substitute

ALCOHOLIC BEVERAGES — See **LIQUOR** or **VERMOUTH** or **WINE**.

ALLSPICE — any amount — *Use one of the following spices, starting with one-half the quantity specified and adding more, as necessary, to taste:*
- ground cinnamon
- ground nutmeg
- ground cloves
- ground cinnamon, cloves and nutmeg in equal amounts

ALMONDS — See also **NUTS**.

| | any amount | • equal amount hazelnuts |
| | 2 tablespoons ground | • ¼ teaspoon almond extract (for flavoring only) |

ANCHOVY — I fillet — • ½ teaspoon anchovy paste

ANCHOVY PASTE — ½ teaspoon — *Use one of the following:*
- I anchovy fillet, mashed
- ½ teaspoon shrimp paste

ANGEL HAIR PASTA — See **PASTA, rods and ribbons (thin).**

Ingredient Specified	Amount	Substitute
ANISE		
• leaf	any amount	*Use one of the following, starting with one-half the quantity specified and adding more, as necessary, to taste:* • fennel leaf • dill leaf • cumin
• seed (aniseed)	any amount	*Use one of the following, starting with one-half the quantity specified and adding more, as necessary, to taste:* • fennel seed • caraway seed • star anise • chervil • a few drops of anise extract per teaspoon specified
ANNATTO SEEDS	any small amount	*Use one of the following:* • pinch of paprika (for color, not flavor) • equal amount of saffron

Ingredient Specified	Amount	Substitute
APPLE		
• **fresh**	I apple chopped *or* I cup chopped	• I cup chopped, firm pears + I tablespoon lemon juice • I cup reconstituted dried apples
• **dried**	I cup rehydrated any amount	• I fresh apple, chopped • equal amount dried pear
• **in pie**	5-7 tart apples	• 5 cups sliced pie apples, drained (2 20-ounce cans)
APPLE PIE SPICE	I teaspoon	• ¹⁄₂ teaspoon ground cinnamon + ¹⁄₄ teaspoon ground nutmeg + ¹⁄₈ teaspoon ground allspice & dash of ground cloves or ginger
APRICOT		
• **fresh**	any amount chopped	• equal amount reconstituted dried apricot, peach or nectarine
• **dried**	any amount	• equal amount dried peach
ARBORIO RICE — See RICE.		
ARTICHOKE (globe)	any amount	• equal amount Jerusalem artichoke or hearts of palm
ARROWROOT	2 teaspoons	***Use one of the following:*** • I tablespoon all-purpose flour • ¹⁄₂ tablespoon cornstarch, potato starch or rice starch
ARUGULA — See GREENS, SALAD (spicy).		

SUBSTITUTIONS

Ingredient Specified	Amount	Substitute
BACON	any amount	• smoked sausage • turkey bacon • *comparable amount Canadian bacon; boiled, baked or smoked ham (lower-fat alternatives)*
	I slice	• I tablespoon bacon bits
BACON BITS	I tablespoon	• I slice bacon, crumbled or chopped
BAKING POWDER • **double acting**	I teaspoon	***Use one of the following:*** • ¼ teaspoon baking soda + ½ teaspoon cream of tartar • ¼ teaspoon baking soda + ½ cup buttermilk, sour milk or yogurt (to replace ½ cup liquid in recipe) • ¼ teaspoon baking soda + ¼ cup molasses (reduce liquid in recipe by ¼ cup; adjust sweeteners) • 2 teaspoons quick-acting baking powder
	for each cup of flour in a recipe	• 2 teaspoons cream of tartar + I teaspoon baking soda +½ teaspoon salt
• **single acting**	I teaspoon	• ¾ teaspoon double-acting baking powder
BANANA • **fresh** • **dried**	any amount any amount	• equal amount plantain (if for baking, mashing or frying) • equal amount dried coconut • equal amount any other dried fruit

Ingredient Specified	Amount	Substitute
BARLEY	any amount	• equal amount brown rice
• groats	any amount	• equal amount barley grits
• grits	any amount	• equal amount buckwheat or hominy grits
BASIL		
• dried	I teaspoon	*Use one of the following:* • I tablespoon chopped fresh basil • I tablespoon chopped fresh summer savory
	any amount	*Use one of the following dried herbs, starting with one-half the quantity specified and adding more, as necessary, to taste:* • marjoram • oregano • thyme • tarragon
• fresh	I tablespoon	• I teaspoon dried basil
BASMATI RICE — See RICE.		
BAY LEAF	any amount	• Fresh and dried bay leaves are generally interchangeable.
	I whole leaf	• ¼ teaspoon crushed bay leaf
	any amount	• equal amount thyme

Ingredient Specified	Amount	Substitute
BEANS, dried	any amount	***Use equal amount of substitute:***
• chickpeas (garbanzo beans)		• broad beans
• fava beans		• baby lima beans or soybeans
• flageolet		• white kidney or great Northern beans
• great Northern beans		• any white beans
• kidney beans		• pink, pinto or red beans
• lentils		• yellow split peas
• lima beans		• soybeans or fava beans
• mung beans		• split peas
• navy beans		• flageolet, great Northern or pea beans
• pea beans		• navy or white beans
• pink beans		• kidney, pinto or red beans
• pinto beans		• kidney, pink or red beans
• red beans		• kidney, pink or pinto beans
• soybeans		• fava or lima beans or green peas
• split peas		• lentil or mung beans
• white beans		• flageolet, great Northern, navy or pea beans
BEANS, edible pod (e.g., snap beans)	any amount	***Substitute freely in equal amounts among the following:*** • Chinese long beans (yard-long beans) • green beans • haricots vert • wax beans

Ingredient Specified	Amount	Substitute
BEANS, fresh-shelled • **cranberry beans** • **fava beans** • **lima beans**	any amount	***Use equal amount of substitute:*** • fava or lima beans • cranberry or lima beans • fava beans
BEANS, fresh	2 cups	• 9-10 ounce package frozen beans
BEEF • **ground** • **fresh**	1 pound any amount	• 1 pound ground pork, veal or lamb • *1 pound ground turkey or chicken (lower-fat alternatives)* • equal amount venison, veal, pork, chicken or turkey

FOOD FAQs QUICK ANSWER

Canned beans can be substituted for dried beans in cooking. If the recipe calls for ¾ cup of dried beans (before soaking and cooking), substitute a 16-ounce can of beans, drained and rinsed.

SUBSTITUTIONS

Ingredient Specified	Amount	Substitute
BEEF BROTH — See **BROTH.**		
BEETS		
• in recipes	any amount	• equal amount sliced or chopped carrots
• in salad	any amount	• equal amount sliced tomato
BEET GREENS — See **GREENS, TANGY (bitter).**		
BISCUIT MIX	I cup	• I cup flour + I ½ teaspoons baking powder + ½ teaspoon salt + I tablespoon shortening
BOUILLON	I teaspoon granulated	• I bouillon cube
		• I bouillon envelope
BOURBON — See **LIQUOR.**		
BRANDY — See **LIQUOR.**		
BRAZIL NUTS — See also **NUTS.**		
	any amount	• 3 times as many macadamia nuts

Ingredient Specified	Amount	Substitute
BREADCRUMBS	I cup fine dry	***Use one of the following:*** • I ⅓ cups soft breadcrumbs • ¾ cup fine cracker or cereal crumbs • 3-4 sandwich-size slices crisp dry bread, crushed • 2 cups rolled oats • I cup flour
• **as topping for casserole**		• *wheat germ (lower-fat alternative)*
BROCCOLI	any amount	• equal amount cauliflower
BROTH (or STOCK)		
• **beef**	I cup	• I teaspoon beef extract blended with I cup boiling water • I beef bouillon cube or I teaspoon granules or I envelope beef bouillon dissolved in I cup of boiling water
• **chicken**	I cup	• I chicken bouillon cube or I teaspoon granules or I envelope chicken bouillon dissolved in I cup of boiling water
• **fish**	I cup	• I cup bottled clam juice • ½ cup chicken broth + ½ cup water
BROWN SUGAR — See **SUGAR, BROWN.**		
BRUSSELS SPROUTS	any amount	• equal amount broccoli flowerets

SUBSTITUTIONS

Ingredient Specified	Amount	Substitute
BUCKWHEAT		
• flour	any amount	• equal amount whole-wheat flour • equal amount all-purpose flour • equal amount other non-wheat flour
• grits	any amount	• equal amount barley or hominy grits
• groats	any amount	• equal amount kasha
BULGHUR	any amount	• equal amount cracked wheat
BUTTER		
• for baking	1 cup	**Use one of the following:** • 1 cup regular margarine • 1 cup vegetable shortening • *1 cup unsweetened applesauce (lower-fat alternative)* • *1 cup fat-free cream cheese (lower-fat alternative)*
• for cooking (not for baking)	1 cup	• 1 cup vegetable oil • $^7/_8$ cup vegetable or animal shortening + $^1/_2$ teaspoon salt • $^3/_4$ cup strained bacon or chicken fat • 1 cup regular margarine • $^1/_2$ cup butter + $^1/_2$ cup vegetable oil
• salted	1 stick	• 1 stick unsalted + $^3/_8$ teaspoon salt
• stick	1 tablespoon	• 1$^1/_3$ tablespoons whipped butter (for any quantity specified, increase by $^1/_3$) (not for baking)

B

C

Ingredient Specified	Amount	Substitute

BUTTERMILK — See **MILK**.

CABBAGE

• **head cabbage** — any amount — • Red and green head cabbage are generally interchangeable.
• equal amount Savoy cabbage

• **Nappa cabbage** — any amount — • equal amount head cabbage

CANNELLONI — See **PASTA, stuffed**.

CANTALOUPE — See **MELON**.

CAPERS — any amount — *Use one of the following:*
• equal amount pickled mild green peppers
• equal amount chopped green olives
• equal amount chopped dill pickles

CAPPELLINI — See **PASTA, rods and ribbons (thin)**.

CARAWAY SEEDS — any amount — *Use one of the following spices, starting with one-half the quantity specified and adding more, as necessary, to taste:*
• anise seed (aniseed)
• fennel seeds
• cumin

SUBSTITUTIONS

Ingredient Specified	Amount	Substitute
CARDAMOM		
• ground	any amount	***Use one of the following spices, starting with one-half the quantity specified and adding more, as necessary, to taste:***
		• cinnamon
		• nutmeg
		• ginger
		• coriander seeds
		• mace
• pods	10 whole pods	• 1 ½ teaspoons ground cardamom
CARROTS		
• in recipes	any amount	• equal amount parsnips or baby white turnips
• in salad	any amount	• equal amount radish
CASHEW NUTS — See also **NUTS.**		
	any amount	• equal amount pine nuts or peanuts
CATSUP — See **KETCHUP.**		
CAULIFLOWER	any amount	• equal amount kohlrabi
		• equal amount broccoli

Ingredient Specified	Amount	Substitute
CAYENNE PEPPER	any amount	*Use one of the following, starting with one-half the quantity specified and adding more, as necessary, to taste:* • ground dried chili pepper • paprika (Hungarian or other pungent paprika) • chili powder • red pepper flakes • 4 drops hot pepper sauce per ¹/₈ teaspoon

FOOD FAQs QUICK ANSWER

In substituting one spice for another, your personal taste preferences are most important. As a rule, no two spices will taste the same in a cooked dish, though many of them will provide an excellent taste experience. Spices listed in this book as substitutes are those that come closest to resembling the taste and texture of the spice specified.

SUBSTITUTIONS

Ingredient Specified	Amount	Substitute
CELERY	any amount	*Use equal amount of one of the following:* • jicama • fennel stalks • green bell pepper • Belgian endive
CELERY ROOT (CELERIAC)	any amount	*Use equal amount of one of the following:* • kohlrabi • turnip • celery
CELERY SEED	1 teaspoon	• 1 tablespoon finely chopped celery leaves • ½ teaspoon dill seed
CHEESE • **firm cheese**		*Substitute freely among choices in each of the following groups:* • gruyère • Jarlsberg • Swiss
• **firm cheese**		• Monterey jack • Muenster • Port Salut • string cheese

Ingredient Specified	Amount	Substitute

CHEESE, *continued*

- **firm cheese**
  - American
  - cheddar
  - Cheshire
  - colby
  - longhorn

- **hard cheese**
  - asiago
  - manchego
  - Parmesan
  - pecorino
  - Romano

- **hard cheese**
  - edam
  - fontina
  - Gouda

- **semisoft cheese**
  - mozzarella
  - provolone

- **semisoft cheese**
  - blue
  - Gorgonzola
  - Roquefort
  - Stilton

SUBSTITUTIONS

Ingredient Specified	Amount	Substitute
CHEESE, *continued*		
• **soft cheese**		• cottage cheese • cream cheese (see also **CHEESE, CREAM**) • farmers cheese • Neufchâtel • ricotta (see also **CHEESE, RICOTTA**) • yogurt cheese
• **soft cheese**		• brinza • chevré • feta • ricotta (see also **CHEESE, RICOTTA**)
CHEESE, CREAM	8 ounces	*Use one of the following:* • 8 ounces cottage cheese, drained, blended with cream, milk and/or a little butter to achieve desired consistency • 8 ounces lowfat cottage cheese blended with ¼ cup margarine • 4 ounces ricotta cheese + 4 ounces plain yogurt • *8 ounces Neufchâtel (lower-fat alternative)* • *8 ounces ricotta cheese with a little vanilla extract, superfine sugar and grated lemon rind (lower-fat alternative)* • *8 ounces yogurt cheese (lower-fat alternative)*

Ingredient Specified	Amount	Substitute
CHEESE, RICOTTA	1 cup	• 1 cup cottage cheese + 1 tablespoon skim milk, blended until smooth
CHERRIES		
• fresh	1 pound	• 3 ounces dried cherries (generally acceptable when cherries are one ingredient among many in a recipe)
• dried	3 ounces	• 1 pound fresh cherries
	any amount	• equal amount dried cranberries or dried apricots
		• equal amount raisins or currants
CHERVIL LEAVES	any amount	• equal amount tarragon leaves
		• equal amount fresh parsley
CHESTNUTS		
• dried	3 ounces	• 1 cup fresh chestnuts
• fresh	1 cup	• 3 ounces dried chestnuts, rehydrated
CHICKEN	1 cup cooked and diced	• 10-ounce can of chicken, drained
	any amount	• equal amount cooked and diced turkey
		• *equal amount extra-firm tofu (lower-fat alternative)*
CHICKEN BROTH — See **BROTH.**		

Ingredient Specified	Amount	Substitute
CHICKPEAS (GARBANZO BEANS) — See **BEANS, dried.**		
CHICORY (CURLY ENDIVE) — See **GREENS, SALAD (spicy).**		
CHILI OIL (hot Chinese)	any amount	• equal amount dark sesame oil with dash of cayenne pepper or pinch of hot pepper flakes
CHILI PASTE	any amount	• equal amount mashed fresh chilis (or to taste)
• **Chinese**	any amount	*Use one of the following:* • equal amount Indonesian chili sambal • equal amount Vietnamese garlic-chili paste • equal amount harissa • hot pepper flakes (start with ¼ amount specified) • dried red pepper (start with ¼ amount specified)
• **Vietnamese**	any amount	*Use one of the following:* • equal amount Indonesian chili sambal • equal amount Chinese chili paste • equal amount harissa • hot pepper flakes (start with ¼ amount specified) • dried red pepper (start with ¼ amount specified)

Ingredient Specified	Amount	Substitute

CHILI PEPPER — See specific dried and fresh chili pepper varieties below.

• **canned**	any amount	• equal amount fresh chili
• **hot**	I small	***Use one of the following:***
		• ¼-½ teaspoon cayenne pepper
		• ½ teaspoon hot pepper flakes
		• ⅛-¼ teaspoon Tabasco Sauce
		• ½ teaspoon hot chili paste
• **mild**	I small	• I tablespoon ground chili powder
• **dried peppers**	any amount	***Substitute freely among choices in each of the following groups:***
· **hot**		• cayenne
		• chili de arbol
		• habanero
		• pequin
· **mild**		• ancho
		• mulato
		• pasilla
· **mild**		• California
		• cascabel
		• guajillo
		• New Mexican

SUBSTITUTIONS

Ingredient Specified	Amount	Substitute

CHILI PEPPER, *continued*

- **fresh peppers**
  - · **hot**

Substitute freely among choices in each of the following groups:
- cayenne
- cherry pepper
- Fresno
- habanero
- jalapeño
- serrano
- yellow wax or guero

  - · **mild**
- Anaheim
- banana pepper
- pepperoncino
- poblano

- **large pepper (to stuff)**

Substitute freely among the following:
- Anaheim
- New Mexican
- poblano

CHILI POWDER   1 teaspoon
- dash of bottled hot pepper sauce + ½ teaspoon combination of oregano and cumin (add more if needed for taste)
- ⅛ teaspoon ground cayenne pepper

Ingredient Specified	Amount	Substitute
CHILI SAMBAL, Indonesian	any amount	• equal amount Chinese chili paste
CHILI SAUCE	1 cup	• 1 cup tomato sauce + $\frac{1}{2}$ cup sugar + 2 tablespoons vinegar [+ $\frac{1}{4}$ teaspoon ground cloves, optional] (for use in cooked mixtures)
• Szechuan	1 teaspoon	• $\frac{1}{2}$ teaspoon minced garlic + $\frac{1}{8}$ teaspoon crushed red pepper
CHIVES	any amount	• equal amount chopped scallions or green onion tops • one-third amount dried chives
CHOCOLATE • semisweet	1 ounce	*Use one of the following:* • 3 tablespoons semisweet chocolate pieces • 1 tablespoon unsweetened cocoa powder + 1 tablespoon sugar and 1 tablespoon shortening • $\frac{1}{2}$ ounce unsweetened chocolate + 1 tablespoon granulated sugar • 1 ounce bittersweet chocolate
• sweet	4 ounces	• $\frac{1}{4}$ cup unsweetened cocoa powder + $\frac{1}{3}$ cup sugar + 3 tablespoons shortening • 4 ounces unsweetened chocolate + $\frac{1}{3}$ cup sugar

Ingredient Specified	Amount	Substitute
CHOCOLATE, *continued*		
• **unsweetened**	1 ounce	*Use one of the following*: • 3 tablespoons unsweetened cocoa powder + 1 tablespoon butter, margarine or vegetable oil • 2 ounces bittersweet chocolate less 1 tablespoon of sugar in recipe • *3 tablespoons carob powder + 2 tablespoons water (lower-fat alternative)* • *3 tablespoons unsweetened cocoa powder + 2 tablespoons water (lower-fat alternative)*
CILANTRO (leaf) — See also **CORIANDER** for seed.		
• **fresh**	any amount	• equal amount fresh parsley or basil
CINNAMON, ground	1 teaspoon	• 3½" cinnamon stick, ground
	any amount	*Use one of the following spices, starting with one-half the amount specified and adding more, as necessary, for taste:* • nutmeg • allspice • cardamom • cloves
CLAM JUICE	1 cup	• ½ cup chicken broth + ½ cup water

Ingredient Specified	Amount	Substitute
CLAMS		• Various varieties of clams are generally interchangeable as cooked meat in recipes.
• fresh	1½-2 dozen shucked *or* 1 cup clam meat	• 2 cans (7½-ounces) minced clams
	any amount	• equal amount mussels, oysters or scallops
CLOVES		
• ground	any amount	*Use one of the following spices, starting with one-half the amount specified and adding more, as necessary, for taste:* • allspice • cinnamon • nutmeg • ginger • mace
• whole	1 teaspoon	• ¾ teaspoon ground cloves
COCOA POWDER	¼ cup	• 1 ounce (1 square) unsweetened chocolate (decrease fat in recipe by ½ tablespoon)
COCONUT		
• fresh	2 cups	• 1⅓ cups flaked coconut
• grated	1 cup	• 1⅓ cups flaked coconut

SUBSTITUTIONS

Ingredient Specified	Amount	Substitute
COCONUT CREAM	I cup	• I cup light cream + ¼ teaspoon coconut extract • I cup light cream
COCONUT MILK	I cup	*Use one of the following*: • 3 tablespoons canned cream of coconut + hot water or lowfat milk to equal I cup • I cup milk beaten with 3 tablespoons grated coconut • I cup whole milk [+ I teaspoon coconut flavoring, optional] • I cup whipping cream + ½ teaspoon *each* coconut extract and sugar • *I cup evaporated skim milk or plain nonfat yogurt + I tablespoon dried coconut + ¼ teaspoon almond extract (lower-fat alternative)*
COFFEE	½ cup strong brewed	• I teaspoon instant coffee in ½ cup water
COGNAC — See **LIQUOR**.		
COLLARD GREENS — See **GREENS, TANGY (bitter)**.		
CONFECTIONERS' SUGAR — See **SUGAR, POWDERED**.		
COOKIE CRUMBS	any amount	• Substitute freely by volume among chocolate wafers, vanilla wafers, gingersnaps and graham crackers.

Ingredient Specified	Amount	Substitute
CORIANDER (seed) — See also **CILANTRO** for leaf.		
	any amount	• equal amount ground coriander
		• equal amount ground cardamom
CORN	any amount	• Fresh and frozen corn kernels can be used interchangeably in equal measure.

FOOD FAQs QUICK ANSWER

You can be creative when considering substitutes for crumbs specified in your recipes. For cracker crumbs, use flavored crumbs, such as onion or cheese crackers, or substitute matzoh for soda crackers, or use cereal flakes; for sweeter crumbs, consider vanilla wafers instead of graham crackers; for dried bread crumbs, substitute whole wheat bread for white or sourdough bread.

SUBSTITUTIONS

Ingredient Specified	Amount	Substitute
CORN SYRUP	I cup	• I¼ cups granulated or packed brown sugar + ¼ cup liquid (use liquid called for in recipe)
• **dark**	I cup	*Use one of the following:* • ¾ cup light corn syrup + ¼ cup light molasses • I cup light corn syrup • I¼ cups dark brown sugar + 3-4 tablespoons water
• **light**	I cup	• I¼ cups granulated white or packed brown sugar + ⅓ cup water, boiled together until syrupy • I cup dark corn syrup • I cup honey
CORNMEAL	any amount	• White, yellow and blue cornmeal can be substituted for one another.
CORNSTARCH **(for thickening)**	I tablespoon	*Use one of the following:* • 2 tablespoons all-purpose flour • I tablespoon potato or rice flour • 4 teaspoons quick-cooking tapioca • 2 teaspoons arrowroot

Ingredient Specified	Amount	Substitute
CRAB	any amount	• Various types and species of crab may be used interchangeably in equal volume.
		• equal amount of scallops, shrimp or lobster
• **fresh meat**	1 cup	• 1-1¼ cans (6-ounce) crabmeat, drained
CRACKER CRUMBS	¾ cup	• 1 cup dry bread crumbs
• **graham cracker**	1 cup	• 1 cup vanilla wafer crumbs

FOOD FAQs QUICK ANSWER

Game birds or specialty poultry species, such as duck, goose, Cornish hens, squab, etc., are generally interchangeable with one another in recipes. For less fatty substitutes, consider using chicken or turkey.

SUBSTITUTIONS

Ingredient Specified	Amount	Substitute
CRANBERRIES		
• **fresh**	any amount	• equal amount frozen cranberries
• **dried**	any amount	• equal amount raisins or dried cherries
CRAYFISH	any amount	• equal amount of shrimp or lobster
CREAM		
• **crème fraîche**	1 cup	*Use one of the following:* • ½ cup *each* sour cream and heavy cream • 1 cup heavy cream + 3 tablespoons buttermilk (cover; let stand 12 hours) • *1 cup yogurt cheese made from lowfat or nonfat yogurt (for use in sauces) (lower-fat alternative)*
• **half & half (in cooked products)**	1 cup	*Use one of the following:* • ⅞ cup milk + 1½ tablespoons melted butter or margarine • ½ cup light cream + ½ cup whole milk
• **heavy (for use in recipes; not for whipping)**	1 cup	*Use one of the following:* • ¾ cup milk + ⅓ cup melted butter or margarine • 1 cup light cream • ⅔ cup evaporated milk • *1 cup evaporated skim milk (lower-fat alternative)* • *2 teaspoons cornstarch or 1 tablespoon flour whisked into 1 cup nonfat milk (lower-fat alternative)*

Ingredient Specified	Amount	Substitute

CREAM, *continued*

• light (coffee cream)   I cup

Use one of the following:
- $^7/_8$ cup whole milk + 3 tablespoons butter or margarine
- I cup half & half cream
- $^1/_2$ cup evaporated milk or heavy cream + $^1/_2$ cup milk

• sour   I cup

Use one of the following:
- I $^1/_2$ tablespoons vinegar + sweet cream or milk to fill I cup (let stand 5 minutes)
- $^1/_2$ cup chilled evaporated milk whipped with I tablespoon white vinegar
- $^7/_8$ cup plain yogurt or buttermilk + 3 tablespoons melted butter
- $^3/_4$ cup sour milk, buttermilk or plain yogurt + $^1/_3$ cup melted butter (for baking)
- I cup cottage cheese (or cottage cheese mixed with plain yogurt to equal I cup) + 2 tablespoons milk + I tablespoon lemon juice, blended well
- I tablespoon lemon juice + evaporated milk to fill I cup (let stand 5 minutes)
- *I cup lowfat cottage cheese or part skim ricotta cheese + nonfat yogurt (or buttermilk) to achieve desired consistency (lower-fat alternative)*
- *I cup lowfat cottage cheese + 2 tablespoons skim milk + I tablespoon lemon juice (lower-fat alternative)*
- *I cup lowfat or nonfat yogurt (lower-fat alternative)*
- *I cup soft tofu (lower-fat alternative)*

SUBSTITUTIONS

Ingredient Specified	Amount	Substitute
CREAM, *continued*		
• **whipping** **(light whipping)**	I cup	***Not to be whipped (for use in cooking and baking):*** • ¾ cup whole milk + ⅓ cup melted butter • I cup half-and-half cream
	Yield: 2 cups whipped	***To be whipped:*** • 2 cups whipped dessert topping • ⅔ cup well-chilled evaporated milk, whipped • 2 cups frozen whipped dessert topping • *I cup nonfat dry milk powder whipped with I cup ice water (lower-fat alternative)* • *½ cup nonfat yogurt + ½ cup part-skim ricotta cheese + 2 tablespoons honey, mixed together (lower-fat alternative)*

CREAM CHEESE — See **CHEESE, CREAM.**

CREAM SAUCE	I ½ cups	• I can condensed cream-style soup + ¼ cup liquid

CRUMBS — See **BREADCRUMBS** and **CRACKER CRUMBS.**

CUCUMBER	any amount	• Regular field grown, hothouse (also known as greenhouse, burpless, English, European) and Japanese cucumbers are generally interchangeable in equal measure.

Ingredient Specified	Amount	Substitute
CUMIN		
• ground	any amount	• equal amount cumin seed
		Use one of the following spices, starting with one-half the amount specified and adding more, as necessary, for taste:
		• chili powder
		• turmeric
		• fennel seed
		• combination of 1 part anise seed to 2 parts caraway seed
• seed	any amount	• equal amount ground cumin
CURRANTS, dried	any amount	*Use one of the following:*
		• equal amount chopped raisins
		• equal amount finely chopped soft prunes or dates
DAIKON	any amount	*Use one of the following:*
		• jicama
		• radish
DASHI	1 cup	*Use one of the following:*
		• 1 cup delicate fish stock
		• ½ cup clam juice + ½ cup water

SUBSTITUTIONS

Ingredient Specified	Amount	Substitute
DATES	any amount	• Fresh and dried dates are generally interchangeable. • equal amount raisins, figs or prunes

DILL
  • leaf
    · fresh

	Amount	Substitute
· fresh	I tablespoon	• I teaspoon dried dill
	any amount	*Use one of the following fresh herbs in equal amount:* • basil • oregano • parsley • rosemary
· dried	any amount	*Use one of the following dried herbs in equal amount:* • basil • oregano • rosemary • tarragon
• seeds	any amount	*Use one of the following seeds, starting with one-half the amount specified and adding more, as necessary, for taste:* • caraway seeds • celery seeds

Ingredient Specified	Amount	Substitute
EGG	1 egg	*Use one of the following:*
		• 2 egg yolks + 1 tablespoon cold water (in baking)
		• 2 tablespoons liquid + 2 tablespoons flour + ½ tablespoon shortening + ½ teaspoon baking powder (in baking)
		• 3½ tablespoons frozen egg, thawed
		• 2 egg yolks (for thickening custards and sauces)
		• 1 teaspoon vegetable oil + 4 teaspoons water + 1 egg white
		• 2 tablespoons mayonnaise (in cake batter)
		• *2 egg whites (lower-fat alternative)*
		• *¼ cup egg substitute (lower-fat alternative)*
	2 eggs	• *3 egg whites (lower-fat alternative)*
	3 eggs	• *5 egg whites (lower-fat alternative)*

FOOD FAQs QUICK ANSWER

The standard egg size used in recipes is *large*. To substitute another egg size for large, use this chart:

Large	Extra Large	Medium	Small
1	1	1	1
2	2	2	3
3	3	3	4
4	4	5	5

SUBSTITUTIONS

Ingredient Specified	Amount	Substitute
EGG WHITE	1 white	• 2 tablespoons frozen egg white, thawed
	2 whites	• 1 egg (for baking; not if egg whites are to be whipped)
EGG YOLK	1 yolk	• 1 tablespoon frozen egg yolk, thawed
	2 yolks	• 1 whole egg (for thickening custards and sauces)
EGG NOODLES — See **NOODLES.**		
EGGPLANT	any amount	• All varieties of eggplant are generally interchangeable in equal measure, though Japanese eggplant is sweeter and more delicate than Italian (or purple) eggplant, and Asian eggplant is more bitter.
ELBOW MACARONI — See **PASTA, tubes.**		
ENDIVE — See **GREENS, SALAD (spicy).**		
ESCAROLE — See **GREENS, SALAD (spicy).**		
ESPRESSO POWDER	any amount	• equal amount instant coffee crystals pulverized into fine powder
EVAPORATED MILK — See **MILK, evaporated.**		
EXTRACT (e.g., almond, vanilla)	½ teaspoon	• 1 or 2 drops oil of same flavor

Ingredient Specified	Amount	Substitute

FARFALLE — See **PASTA, shapes.**

FAT — See also specific fats and oils.

• **baking**	any amount	• equal amount applesauce or puréed prunes + beaten egg whites substituted for ½ of butter specified (lower-fat alternative)
• **basting**	any amount	**Use one of the following in equal measure:** • wine (lower-fat alternative) • stock or broth (lower-fat alternative) • fruit juice (lower-fat alternative)
• **sautéeing**	any amount	• 4 times as much stock, wine, vinegar, juice or water, sautéed until liquid evaporates (lower-fat alternative)

FENNEL (also called **ANISE**)

• **bulb**	8 ounce bulb	• 3 stalks celery chopped
	1 cup finely chopped	• 1 teaspoon crushed fennel seeds (for flavor; not when fennel is used as a vegetable)
• **leaf or seed**	any amount	**Use one of the following, starting with one-half the quantity specified and adding more, as necessary, to taste:** • anise seed (aniseed) • caraway seed

---

FIDEO — See **PASTA, rods and ribbons (thin).**

Ingredient Specified	Amount	Substitute
FIGS	any amount chopped	• equal amount raisins, dried currants or finely chopped dates
FILBERTS — See **HAZELNUTS/FILBERTS.**		
FINES HERBES	2 tablespoons	• 1 teaspoon *each* dried thyme, oregano, marjoram, parsley and chervil + ½ teaspoon dried chives + ¼ teaspoon *each* dried sage and tarragon

FOOD FAQs QUICK ANSWER

Fresh, frozen and canned vegetables are generally interchangeable in recipes. For the equivalent of 2 cups of fresh, cut-up vegetables, substitute 2 cups of frozen, loose-pack vegetables, cooked and drained, or 1 can (16 ounces) of vegetable, drained.

Ingredient Specified	Amount	Substitute
FISH		*Substitute freely among choices in each group:*

- **mild flavor**
  - · **delicate texture**
    - Alaska pollock
    - flounder
    - orange roughy
    - skate
    - sole
    - weakfish
  - · **medium firm texture**
    - California halibut
    - catfish
    - Chilean sea bass
    - cod
    - haddock
    - perch
    - pike
    - porgy
    - red snapper
    - rockfish
    - salmon, pink
    - striped bass, farmed
    - tilapia

Ingredient Specified	Amount	Substitute

FISH, mild flavor, *continued*

Substitute freely among choices in each group:

· **firm texture**

- grouper
- kingclip
- lingcod
- monkfish
- Pacific halibut
- tautog
- wolffish

• **moderate flavor**
  · **delicate texture**

- butterfish
- hake
- whiting

· **medium firm texture**

- Atlantic pollock
- carp
- drum, red/blue
- mahi-mahi
- mullet
- salmon, chum/silverbright
- sea bass, black/white
- striped bass, wild
- trout

· **firm texture**

- pompano
- shark
- sturgeon

Ingredient Specified	Amount	Substitute

FISH, *continued*
- **full flavor**   *Substitute freely among choices in each group:*
  - **delicate texture**
    - anchovy
    - herring
    - sardine
  - **medium firm texture**
    - barracuda
    - bluefish
    - sablefish
    - salmon, coho (silver)/king (chinook)/sockeye
    - yellowtail and other jacks
  - **firm texture**
    - mackerels
    - opah
    - swordfish
    - tuna, albacore/bonito/yellowfin (ahi)

FISH SAUCE   I tablespoon
- 2½ teaspoons Chinese soy sauce + ½ teaspoon anchovy paste
- I tablespoon anchovy paste

FISH STOCK — See BROTH.

FIVE-SPICE POWDER   any amount
- equal amount ground star anise

SUBSTITUTIONS

Ingredient Specified	Amount	Substitute
FLOUR (for baking)		
• all-purpose	I cup	*Use one of the following:* • I cup + 2 tablespoons sifted cake flour • I cup self-rising flour (omit baking powder and salt from recipe) • I cup minus I tablespoon pre-sifted flour • I cup finely milled whole grain or graham flour • I cup + 2 tablespoons coarsely milled whole grain or graham flour • ¾ cup gluten flour • ⅞ cup rice flour • I½ cups rye flour • ½ cup barley flour • I cup corn meal • I½ cups oat flour
	I cup sifted	• I cup minus 2 tablespoons unsifted all-purpose flour
• bread	any amount	• equal amount all-purpose flour
• buckwheat	any amount	• equal amount whole-wheat flour
• cake	I cup sifted	• I cup minus 2 tablespoons (⅞ cup) stirred or sifted all-purpose flour or white flour
• graham	I cup	• I cup whole wheat flour
• oat	any amount	• equal amount whole-wheat flour
• pastry	I cup	• I cup minus 2 tablespoons (⅞ cup) all-purpose or bread flour • ¾ cup + I tablespoon bread or all-purpose flour + 3 tablespoons cake flour

Ingredient Specified	Amount	Substitute
FLOUR (for baking), *continued*		
• self-rising	I cup	• I cup sifted all-purpose flour + I ½ teaspoons baking powder + ⅛ teaspoon salt
• triticale	any amount	• equal amount whole-wheat flour
• whole wheat	I cup	• 2 tablespoons wheat germ + all-purpose flour to make I cup
		• I cup graham flour
		• I cup barley flour (in quick bread recipes)

Fresh, frozen and canned fruits are generally interchangeable in recipes. For the equivalent of 1½ cups of fresh, cut-up fruit, substitute 1½ cups of frozen, loose-pack fruit, drained, or 1 can (16-20 ounces) of fruit, drained.

SUBSTITUTIONS

Ingredient Specified	Amount	Substitute
FLOUR (for thickening)		
• all-purpose	I tablespoon	***Use one of the following:***
		• I ½ teaspoons cornstarch, arrowroot, potato starch or rice starch
		• I tablespoon quick-cooking tapioca
• potato	I tablespoon	• 2 tablespoons all-purpose flour
FRUIT — See also specific fruits.		
• canned	16-20-ounce can	• I ½ cups cut-up fresh fruit
		• I ½ cups frozen loose-pack fruit, drained
• frozen	10-ounce package	• I ¼ cups cut-up fresh fruit
		• I ¼ cups canned fruit, drained
FRUIT (in pie)		
• fresh	any amount	• equal volume of frozen fruit
FRUIT (to be cooked)		
• berries	any amount	***Substitute freely, by weight, among the following:***
		• blackberries and raspberries
		• blueberries, huckleberries and cranberries
		• currants and gooseberries

Ingredient Specified	Amount	Substitute

FRUIT (to be cooked), *continued*

• bone fruits (central core with small seeds)	any amount	*Substitute freely, by weight, among the following:* • apples • pears • quinces
• citrus fruits	any amount	*Substitute freely, by weight, among the following:* • orange • grapefruit • lemon • lime • tangerine
• stone fruits (single pit)	any amount	*Substitute freely, by weight, among the following:* • apricots • cherries • nectarines • peaches • plums

FRUIT, candied	any amount	• equal amount dried fruit
• peel	I cup	• I teaspoon grated fresh citrus peel + I cup golden raisins

FUSILLI — See **PASTA, shapes.**

SUBSTITUTIONS

Ingredient Specified	Amount	Substitute
GALANGAL **(Siamese ginger)**	any amount	*Use one of the following:* • equal amount fresh gingerroot • $1/3$ quantity ground ginger
GARBANZO BEANS — See **BEANS, dried.**		
GARLIC, fresh	I small clove	*Use one of the following:* • $1/8$ teaspoon garlic powder or dried minced garlic • $1/2$ teaspoon bottled minced garlic • $1/4$ teaspoon garlic juice • $1/4$ teaspoon garlic salt (reduce salt in recipe by $1/8$ teaspoon)
GARLIC POWDER	$1/8$ teaspoon	• I small clove fresh garlic, minced
GARLIC SALT	I teaspoon	• $1/8$ teaspoon garlic powder + $7/8$ teaspoon salt
GELATIN, powdered • **flavored** • **unflavored**	 3 ounces I envelope	 • I tablespoon unflavored (plain) gelatin + 2 cups fruit juice • 4 sheets leaf gelatin

Ingredient Specified	Amount	Substitute
GINGER		
• **fresh gingerroot**	½" piece (of 1½" diameter root) or 1 tablespoon chopped	***Use one of the following:*** • 1 teaspoon ground dried ginger • 1 tablespoon candied (crystallized) ginger, sugar washed off
• **ground**	any amount	***Use one of the following spices, starting with one-half of the quantity specified and adding more, as necessary, to taste:*** • allspice • cinnamon • mace or nutmeg • cardamom • coriander seed • 1 part mace to 2 parts lemon peel
GINGER, candied	1 tablespoon	• ⅛ teaspoon powdered ginger + ⅛ teaspoon sugar

GNOCCHI — See **PASTA, shapes.**

GREEN ONION — See **ONION, GREEN.**

SUBSTITUTIONS

Ingredient Specified	Amount	Substitute
GREENS, SALAD		
• mild	any amount	*Substitute freely among the following:* • butterhead lettuce (Bibb, Boston, etc.) • iceberg lettuce • leaf lettuce • romaine lettuce
• spicy	any amount	*Substitute freely among the following:* • arugula (rocket) • Belgian endive • curly endive (chicory) • escarole • radicchio • watercress
GREENS, TANGY		
• bitter	any amount	*Substitute freely among the following:* • beet greens • collard greens • mustard greens • turnip greens
• sharp	any amount	*Substitute freely among the following:* • kale • spinach • Swiss chard

Ingredient Specified	Amount	Substitute
GRITS	any amount	*Substitute freely among the following:* • barley grits • buckwheat grits • hominy grits
HAM	any amount	*Use one of the following:* • bacon • Canadian bacon
HARISSA (hot sauce)	any amount	*Use one of the following:* • Chinese chili paste to taste • Indonesian chili sambal to taste
HAZELNUTS/FILBERTS — See also **NUTS.**		
	any amount	• equal amount almonds, walnuts, pecans or Brazil nuts
HERBS — See also specific herbs.		
• **fresh**	I tablespoon chopped	*Use one of the following:* • I teaspoon crumbled dried leaf herb • ½ teaspoon dried ground herb

Ingredient Specified	Amount	Substitute
HERBS, *continued* • **dried**		
· **leaf**	any amount	*Use one of the following:* • fresh herb in 3 times the quantity • ground form of herb in ½ quantity
· **ground**	any amount	*Use one of the following:* • fresh herb in 6 times the quantity • dried leaf form in 2 times the quantity
HERBS DE PROVENCE	2 tablespoons	• 4 teaspoons *each* dried thyme and marjoram + 1½ teaspoons dried summer savory + ¼ teaspoon *each* dried rosemary and mint + ⅛ teaspoon fennel seeds + pinch *each* of dried sage and lavender flowers
HOMINY GRITS	any amount	*Substitute freely among the following:* • barley grits • buckwheat grits
HONEY	1 cup	*Use one of the following:* • 1¼ cups granulated sugar + ¼ cup liquid (use liquid called for in recipe) • 1 cup molasses • 1 cup light or dark corn syrup • 1 cup maple syrup

Ingredient Specified	Amount	Substitute

HONEYDEW — See MELON.

HORSERADISH
- **fresh** — 1 tablespoon grated — • 2 tablespoons bottled prepared horseradish
- **bottled (prepared)** — 1 tablespoon — • ½ tablespoon grated fresh horseradish
  - • ½ teaspoon dried (powdered) horseradish

HOT PEPPER SAUCE — 3-4 drops — *Use one of the following:*
- • equal amount any bottled hot sauce
- • ⅛ teaspoon cayenne pepper, hot red pepper flakes or chili powder (add more to taste, if necessary)

HOT RED PEPPER FLAKES — See RED PEPPER FLAKES, HOT.

ITALIAN HERB SEASONING — 2 tablespoons — • ¾ tablespoon dried oregano + 1½ teaspoons dried basil + ¾ teaspoon *each* dried marjoram and dried thyme + ½ teaspoon crushed dried rosemary

JERUSALEM ARTICHOKE — any amount — *Use an equal amount of one of the following:*
- • artichoke heart
- • water chestnut
- • jicama

SUBSTITUTIONS

Ingredient Specified	Amount	Substitute
JICAMA	any amount	*Use an equal amount of one of the following:* • water chestnuts • daikon • turnip
JOB'S TEARS	any amount	• equal amount barley
KALE — See **GREENS, TANGY (sharp).**		
KASHA	any amount	*Use an equal amount of one of the following:* • buckwheat groats • bulghur
KETCHUP (in cooking)	I cup	• I cup tomato sauce + ¼ cup sugar + 2 tablespoons vinegar + ¼ teaspoon ground cloves
KIWI	any amount	• equal amount strawberries drizzled with small amount of lime juice
KOHLRABI	any amount	*Use an equal amount of one of the following:* • turnip • celery root (celeriac) • cauliflower • broccoli stems

Ingredient Specified	Amount	Substitute
LAMB, ground	any amount	• equal amount ground beef or ground pork
LARD	any amount	*Use one of the following:* • 25% more butter or margarine (in baking) • equal amount shortening • equal amount vegetable oil (for frying)

LASAGNA — See **PASTA, rods and ribbons (flat).**

LEEK	½ cup chopped or sliced	*Use one of the following:* • ¼-½ cup onion chopped or sliced • ½ cup shallots or green onions chopped
LEMON CURD	any amount	• equal amount lemon pudding
LEMON JUICE	I teaspoon	*Use one of the following:* • ½ teaspoon malt or other vinegar • I teaspoon lime juice • ½ teaspoon bottled lemon extract • I teaspoon white wine
	juice of I lemon	• 3 tablespoons bottled lemon juice
LEMON PEEL, dried	I teaspoon	*Use one of the following:* • grated peel of I medium lemon • ½ teaspoon lemon extract

SUBSTITUTIONS

Ingredient Specified	Amount	Substitute
LEMON ZEST • **fresh grated**	I teaspoon	***Use one of the following:*** • ½ teaspoon dried lemon peel • I teaspoon lemon marmalade • I teaspoon lime or orange zest • ½ teaspoon lemon extract
LEMONGRASS	I tablespoon *or* 2 stalks finely chopped	• 2 teaspoons finely grated lemon zest
LETTUCE — See **GREENS, SALAD (mild).**		
LIME JUICE	I teaspoon	• I teaspoon lemon juice
LIME ZEST • **fresh grated**	I teaspoon	• I teaspoon lemon or orange zest
LINGUINE — See **PASTA, rods and ribbons (flat).**		
LIQUOR (in cooking) • **brandy**	any amount	• Cognac and other brandies are interchangeable in equal measure. • I part brandy extract + 4 parts water or other liquid • equal amount rum or bourbon • equal measure unsweetened orange juice or apple juice + I teaspoon of corresponding flavored extract or vanilla extract

Ingredient Specified	Amount	Substitute

LIQUOR (in cooking), *continued*

• **bourbon**	any amount	• equal amount whiskey or sherry
	½ cup	• ¼ cup unsweetened fruit juice or broth
	2 tablespoons	• I teaspoon vanilla extract + 2 teaspoons water
• **liqueur**		
· **coffee-flavored (i.e., Kahlua)**	2 tablespoons	• ½-I teaspoon chocolate extract + ½-I teaspoon instant coffee in 2 tablespoons water

Substitute in equal measure among choices in each group:

· **licorice-flavored**		• arak • ouzo • pastis • Pernod • Sambuca
· **orange-flavored**		• curaçao • Cointreau • Grand Marnier
· **raspberry-flavored**		• cassis • chambrod
• **rum**	any amount	• equal amount brandy or cognac • equal measure unsweetened orange juice or apple juice + I teaspoon of corresponding flavored extract or vanilla extract
	½ cup	• ¼ cup unsweetened fruit juice or broth
	2 tablespoons	• ½ to I teaspoon rum or brandy extract in recipes in which liquid amount is not crucial; add water or apple juice, if necessary, to reach specified amount of liquid

SUBSTITUTIONS

Ingredient Specified	Amount	Substitute
LIQUOR (in cooking), *continued*		
• **whiskey**	any amount	• equal amount bourbon or sherry
		• 1 part vanilla extract + 2 parts water
	½ cup	• ¼ cup unsweetened fruit juice or broth
LOBSTER	1 whole fresh	• 2 frozen lobster tails
LOTUS ROOT	any amount	*Use one of the following:*
		• water chestnuts
		• Jerusalem artichoke
LOVAGE, leaves or stalks	any amount	• equal amount celery leaves or stalks
MACARONI — See **PASTA.**		
MACADAMIA NUT	any amount	*Use an equal amount of one of the following:*
		• Brazil nuts
		• pecans
		• walnuts

Ingredient Specified	Amount	Substitute
MACE	any amount	*Use one of the following spices, starting with one-half the amount specified and adding more, as necessary, to taste:* • allspice • cinnamon • ginger • nutmeg • cloves

MADEIRA — See **WINE, heavy.**

MALT VINEGAR — See **VINEGAR, malt.**

MANICOTTI — See **PASTA, stuffed.**

MANGO, fresh or dried	any amount	• equal amount peach or papaya

MAPLE SYRUP		
• **in recipes**	any amount	• equal amount corn syrup
• **for pancakes**	1 cup	• ¾ cup corn syrup or molasses + ¼ cup butter [+ ½ teaspoon maple extract, optional] • 1 cup other fruit syrup

SUBSTITUTIONS

Ingredient Specified	Amount	Substitute

MARGARINE — See also **BUTTER.**

| | 1 cup | *Use one of the following:*
• 1 cup butter
• 1 cup shortening + ¼ teaspoon salt, if desired |
| • diet | 1 cup | • ½ cup butter or stick margarine (not for baking) |

MARJORAM

| • dried | 1 teaspoon | *Use one of the following:*
• 1 tablespoon fresh chopped marjoram
• 1½ teaspoons chopped fresh oregano
• 1 teaspoon dried thyme |
| • fresh | 1 tablespoon chopped | *Use one of the following;*
• 1 teaspoon dried marjoram
• 2 teaspoons chopped fresh oregano
• 1 tablespoon chopped fresh basil leaves |

MARSALA — See **WINE, heavy.**

| **MARSHMALLOWS** | 16 regular (¼ pound) | • 200 (2 cups) miniature marshmallows
• 5 ounces marshmallow cream |
| | 2 ounces miniature | • 8 regular marshmallows
• 2½ ounces marshmallow cream |

Ingredient Specified	Amount	Substitute
MAYONNAISE	I cup	***Use one of the following:*** • I cup sour cream or plain yogurt • I cup cottage cheese puréed in blender • *I cup lowfat yogurt or nonfat sour cream (lower-fat alternative)*
MEAT (ground beef)	I pound	• *I pound ground chicken or turkey (lower-fat alternative)*
MELON	any amount	***Substitute freely, in equal weight or measure, among the following and similar melons:*** • cantaloupe • casaba • cranshaw • honeydew • Persian
	any amount	• equal amount papaya or mango

SUBSTITUTIONS

Ingredient Specified	Amount	Substitute

MILK

Ingredient Specified	Amount	Substitute
• **buttermilk**	1 cup	*Use one of the following:*

- 1 cup plain yogurt
- 1 tablespoon lemon juice or vinegar + whole milk to make 1 cup
- $^2/_3$ cup plain yogurt + $^1/_3$ cup milk
- ½ cup canned milk + ½ cup water + 1 tablespoon vinegar
- 1 cup milk + 1¾ tablespoons cream of tartar
- ¼ cup buttermilk powder + 1 cup water
- 1 cup sour cream
- *1 cup nonfat or lowfat yogurt (lower-fat alternative)*
- *1-2 tablespoons lemon juice or vinegar + nonfat milk to make 1 cup (lower-fat alternative)*
- *2-3 tablespoons plain, nonfat yogurt + nonfat milk to make 1 cup (lower-fat alternative)*

Ingredient Specified	Amount	Substitute
• **sweetened condensed**	14-ounce can	• 1 cup instant nonfat dry milk + $^2/_3$ cup granulated sugar + ½ cup boiling water + 3 tablespoons melted unsalted butter, processed in blender or food processor until smooth

Ingredient Specified	Amount	Substitute
• **evaporated**	1 cup	*Use one of the following:*

- 1 cup half-and-half
- 1 cup heavy cream
- 1 cup whole milk

Ingredient Specified	Amount	Substitute
• **nonfat (skim)**	1 cup	*Use one of the following:*

- $^1/_3$ cup dry nonfat milk solids + ¾ cup water
- ½ cup evaporated skim milk + ½ cup water

Ingredient Specified	Amount	Substitute

MILK, *continued*

• sour — I cup

Use one of the following:
- ½ cup canned milk + ½ cup water + I tablespoon vinegar
- I cup buttermilk or any substitute listed for it
- *I tablespoon lemon juice or white vinegar + whole milk to make I cup (use nonfat milk for lower-fat alternative)*

• whole — I cup

Use one of the following:
- ½ cup whole milk + ½ cup water
- ½ cup evaporated whole milk + ½ cup water
- ½ cup condensed milk + ½ cup water
- I cup nonfat milk [+ 2 teaspoons melted butter, optional]
- ⅓ cup nonfat dry milk + I cup water [+ 2 tablespoons melted butter, optional]
- I cup fruit juice + ½ teaspoon baking soda added to flour (in baking)
- I cup buttermilk + ½ teaspoon baking soda (in baking)

MILLET — any amount

Use one of the following:
- equal amount orzo
- equal amount barley
- equal amount bulghur

Ingredient Specified	Amount	Substitute
MINT		
• **fresh**	1 tablespoon chopped	• 1 teaspoon dried mint
	any amount	*Use an equal amount of one of the following fresh herbs:* • basil • marjoram • rosemary
• **dried**	any amount	*Use one of the following dried herbs, starting with one-half the amount specified and adding more to taste, as necessary:* • basil • marjoram • rosemary
MISO (bean paste)	any amount small amount	• Red, yellow and white miso are generally interchangeable in equal measure. • equal amount tahini or Chinese sesame paste (when only a small amount of miso is required; there is no substitute when miso is predominant flavor)
MOLASSES	1 cup	*Use one of the following:* • 1 cup honey • ¾ cup brown or white sugar + ¼ cup liquid • 1 cup dark corn syrup • 1 cup maple syrup

Ingredient Specified	Amount	Substitute

MOSTACCIOLI — See **PASTA, tubes.**

MUSHROOMS

• dried	3 ounces	• I pound fresh mushrooms
• fresh (cultivated)	I pound	*Use one of the following:* • 8-12 ounces canned mushrooms, drained • 3 ounces dried mushrooms, rehydrated
· brown	any amount	• white mushrooms in slightly larger quantity than recipe specifies
· white	any amount	• brown mushrooms in slightly smaller quantity than recipe specifies
• fresh (wild)	I pound	• 3-4 ounces dried mushrooms, rehydrated
	any amount	• equal amount cultivated fresh mushrooms + ½ ounce dried wild mushrooms

MUSSELS any amount cooked meat *Use equal amount of cooked meat of any of the following:*
- clams
- oysters
- other shellfish

SUBSTITUTIONS

Ingredient Specified	Amount	Substitute
MUSTARD		
• **prepared**		
· **American mustard**	1 tablespoon	• 1 teaspoon dry mustard + 1 tablespoon water, vinegar or white wine • 1 tablespoon prepared horseradish
· **Chinese, hot**	any amount	• equal amount dry mustard prepared with water
· **Dijon**	1 tablespoon	• 1 tablespoon dry mustard + 1 teaspoon water + 1 teaspoon white vinegar + 1 tablespoon mayonnaise + pinch of sugar
• **seeds**	1 teaspoon	*Use one of the following:* • 1½ teaspoons dry mustard • 1½ tablespoons prepared mustard • 1 teaspoon caraway seeds
• **dry** (**in cooked mixtures**)	1 teaspoon	• 1 tablespoon prepared mustard

MUSTARD GREENS — See **GREENS, TANGY (bitter).**

NECTARINE	any amount	• equal amount peach or apricots

NONFAT MILK — See **MILK, nonfat.**

Ingredient Specified	Amount	Substitute
NOODLES		
• **Oriental** (e.g., somen, udon)	any amount	• equal amount fine egg noodles, thin spaghetti, vermicelli or angel hair hair pasta, except for recipes that call for deep-fry
• **Italian style**	any amount	• equal amount any Italian pasta
• **Jewish**	any amount	• equal amount Italian egg noodles
NUTMEG	any amount	*Use one of the following spices, starting with one-half the amount specified and adding more, as necessary, to taste:* • cinnamon • ginger • mace • allspice • cloves
NUTS	any amount	• equal amount Grape Nuts cereal • equal amount rolled oats, browned (for use in baked products)
	½ cup	• *¼ cup toasted nuts (lower-fat alternative)*
	See also specific nuts.	

SUBSTITUTIONS

Ingredient Specified	Amount	Substitute
OATS		
• **bran**	½ cup	• ⅔ cup rolled oats processed in blender or food processor until ground • ½ cup wheat, corn or rice bran
• **flour**	any amount	• equal amount whole-wheat flour
• **groats, raw (in recipes)**	any amount	• equal amount barley
• **quick-cooking rolled**	any amount	• equal amount regular (old-fashioned) rolled oats
• **rolled, regular (old-fashioned)**	any amount	• equal amount quick-cooking rolled oats

FOOD FAQs QUICK ANSWER

Oils are generally interchangeable in equal amounts in cooking, though individual characteristics of oils should be considered. Flavoring oils, such as almond, hazelnut, mustard, dark sesame and walnut oils, which begin to smoke at relatively low temperatures, are not suitable for frying or sautéeing. For these purposes, select a vegetable oil, such as canola, corn, safflower or soy oil, which will smoke at a relatively high temperature.

Ingredient Specified	Amount	Substitute
OIL		
• **for baking**	1 tablespoon	*Use one of the following:*
		• 1 ¼ tablespoons butter or margarine
		• 1 tablespoon mayonnaise (in cake recipes)
	1 cup	• *1 cup unsweetened applesauce (lower-fat alternative)*
• **for basting**	any amount	• *equal amount fruit juice (lower-fat alternative)*
• **for cooking**	2 cups	• 1 pound fat
	any amount	• All cooking oils are generally interchangeable in equal amounts, though some will add their distinctive flavors to foods.
• **flavoring oil**	any amount	• All flavoring oils are generally interchangeable in equal amounts, though each will add its own distinctive flavor to foods.
• **vegetable oil**	any amount	• All vegetable oils are generally interchangeable in equal amounts, though some will add their distinctive flavors to foods.
OKRA, fresh	1 pound	• 2 10-ounce packages frozen okra
	any amount	• equal amount eggplant (not for thickening)
OLIVES	any amount	• All olives are generally interchangeable in recipes in equal amounts, though each will add its own distinctive flavor to foods.

SUBSTITUTIONS

Ingredient Specified	Amount	Substitute
ONION		
• fresh	¼ cup finely chopped *or* I small	*Use one of the following:* • I tablespoon instant minced onion, rehydrated • 1-2 teaspoons onion powder • ¼-½ cup shallots, finely chopped leeks or green onions
• freeze-dried	I teaspoon	• I tablespoon chopped fresh onion
• boiling onion	any amount	• equal amount pearl onion
• pearl onion	any amount	• equal amount boiling onion
ONION, GREEN	¼ cup sliced	• ¼ cup chopped or sliced scallions, leeks, shallots, chives or mild onions
ONION POWDER	I tablespoon	• ¼ cup chopped fresh onion (I small onion)
ORANGE BLOSSOM WATER	any amount	• equal amount white orange flower water, rose water or any other flower water
ORANGE JUICE	from I medium orange	• ¼ cup reconstituted frozen orange juice
ORANGE PEEL (rind)		
• dried	I tablespoon	*Use one of the following:* • grated peel of I medium orange • 2 teaspoons orange extract

Ingredient Specified	Amount	Substitute
ORANGE PEEL, *continued*		
• **fresh**	I teaspoon grated	*Use one of the following:*
		• I teaspoon dried orange peel
		• I teaspoon orange marmalade
		• I teaspoon lemon or lime zest
• **zest**	I teaspoon	• I teaspoon lemon or lime zest
OREGANO		
• **dried**	I teaspoon	• I tablespoon fresh chopped oregano
		• 2 tablespoons fresh chopped marjoram
	any amount	*Use one of the following dried herbs, starting with one-half the quantity specified and adding more, as necessary, to taste:*
		• rosemary
		• marjoram
		• thyme
• **fresh**	I tablespoon chopped	*Use one of the following:*
		• 2 tablespoons chopped fresh marjoram
		• I teaspoon dried oregano
		• I tablespoon chopped fresh thyme
		• I tablespoon chopped fresh basil

ORZO — See **PASTA, salad pasta.**

SUBSTITUTIONS

Ingredient Specified	Amount	Substitute
OYSTER SAUCE	any amount	• equal amount soy sauce
OYSTERS	6-8 medium shucked any amount	• 10-ounce jar of oysters • equal amount scallops, mussels or clams
PAPAYA, fresh or dried	any amount	• equal amount mango • double the quantity specified peaches or nectarines
PAPRIKA	any amount	*Use one of the following, adding more, as necessary, to taste:* • cayenne pepper in ¼ the quantity specified • turmeric with a pinch of cayenne pepper in ½ the quantity specified
PARSLEY • **dried flakes** • **fresh**	 1 tablespoon 3 tablespoons minced	 *Use one of the following:* • 2-3 tablespoons fresh minced parsley • ½ tablespoon dried tarragon *Use one of the following:* • 1 tablespoon dried parsley flakes • 3 tablespoons fresh chopped basil • 3 tablespoons fresh chopped chervil
PARSNIP	any amount	• equal amount carrots • equal amount turnip

Ingredient Specified	Amount	Substitute
PASSION FRUIT	any amount	• equal amount pomegranate, guava or pineapple

PASTA, Italian style — See also **NOODLES** for Oriental style pasta.

• **fresh**	1½ pounds	• 1 pound dried pasta
• **dried**	1 pound	• 1½ pounds fresh pasta
• **rods and ribbons**		
· **flat**	any amount	*Substitute freely, by weight, among the following and other similar pastas:* • bavette • lasagna • linguine
· **thin**	any amount	*Substitute freely, by weight, among the following and other similar pastas:* • angel hair • bucatini • cappellini • fideo • spaghetti • tagliarini • vermicelli

SUBSTITUTIONS

Ingredient Specified	Amount	Substitute

PASTA, Italian style, *continued*

- **salad pasta** — any amount — *Substitute freely, by weight, among the following and other similar pastas:*
  - orzo/riso
  - pastina
  - stellini

- **shapes** — any amount — *Substitute freely, by weight, among the following and other similar pastas:*
  - bowties
  - farfalle
  - fusilli
  - gnocchi
  - rotelle
  - rotini
  - shells

- **stuffed (to be filled)** — any amount — *Substitute freely, by weight, among the following and other similar pastas:*
  - agnolotti
  - cannelloni
  - manicotti
  - ravioli

- **tubes** — any amount — *Substitute freely, by weight, among the following and other similar pastas:*
  - elbow macaroni
  - mostaccioli
  - penne
  - rigatoni
  - ziti

Ingredient Specified	Amount	Substitute
PEACH		
• fresh	any amount	• equal amount nectarine or apricot
• dried	any amount	*Use one of the following:* • equal amount dried nectarine • equal amount dried apricot
PEANUTS	any amount	• equal amount cashews
PEANUT BUTTER	any amount	*Use one of the following:* • equal amount sesame paste (tahini) • equal amount any other nut butter
PEAR		
• fresh or dried	1 cup chopped	• Fresh and reconstituted dried pear can be used interchangeably in equal measure. • 1 cup chopped fresh apples or reconstituted dried apples
• in pies	3 fresh	• 3½ cups canned pear halves
PEAS, edible pod	any amount	*Substitute freely in equal amount among the following:* • sugar peas (snow peas) • sugar snap peas

P

Ingredient Specified	Amount	Substitute
PEAS, SHELL, fresh	any amount	• All fresh or frozen shell peas are interchangeable in equal measure.
	2 cups	• 1 10-ounce package frozen peas
PECANS — See also **NUTS**.		
	any amount	• equal amount walnuts
PENNE — See **PASTA, tubes**.		
PEPPER, CAYENNE — See **CAYENNE PEPPER**.		
PEPPER, CHILI — See **CHILI PEPPER**.		
PEPPER, SWEET (bell)	any amount	***Substitute freely among the following:*** • sweet green pepper • sweet red pepper • sweet yellow pepper
• **roasted**	1 small	• 4-ounce jar pimento, drained
PEPPERCORNS	any amount	• White and black peppercorns may be used interchangeably, though black pepper is stronger than white.

Ingredient Specified	Amount	Substitute
PERSIMMON		
• dried	any amount	• equal amount any other dried fruit
• fresh	any amount	• equal amount plums • equal amount mashed pumpkin (when used in batters)
PHYLLO DOUGH PASTRY LEAVES	any amount	• equal amount strudel dough
PIMENTO	4-ounce jar	• I small red sweet pepper, roasted
PINE NUTS	any amount	• equal amount chopped walnuts or slivered almonds
PINEAPPLE	any amount	• Canned and fresh pineapple are generally interchangeable in equal measure. • equal amount papaya
• dried	any amount	• equal amount dried papaya or mango
PISTACHIO NUTS	any amount	• equal amount pine nuts or blanched almonds
PLANTAIN	any amount	*Use one of the following in equal measure:* • green-tipped bananas • sweet potatoes
POMEGRANATE	any amount	• equal amount passion fruit
• juice	any amount	• equal amount grenadine

SUBSTITUTIONS

Ingredient Specified	Amount	Substitute
PORK		
• fresh	any amount	• equal amount of chicken, lamb, turkey, veal or beef
• ground	½ pound	• ½ pound mild sausage

PORT — See **WINE, heavy.**

POTATO FLOUR — See **FLOUR (for thickening).**

POULTRY SEASONING	I teaspoon	• ¾ teaspoon crushed dried sage + ¼ teaspoon crushed dried thyme or marjoram

POWDERED SUGAR — See **SUGAR, POWDERED.**

PRUNES, dried	½ cup pitted and chopped	*Use one of the following:* • ½ cup raisins • ½ cup pitted dates or dried apricots, chopped
PUMPKIN	any amount mashed	*Use one of the following:* • equal amount cooked, puréed winter squash • equal amount cooked, puréed carrots • equal amount cooked, puréed sweet potato (especially in pies)

P

Q

R

Ingredient Specified	Amount	Substitute
PUMPKIN PIE SPICE	I teaspoon	• ¹/₂ teaspoon ground cinnamon + ¹/₄ teaspoon *each* ground ginger and allspice + ¹/₈ teaspoon ground nutmeg
QUINCE	any amount	*Use one of the following:* • equal amount apples • equal amount pears
QUINOA	any amount	*Use one of the following:* • equal amount white rice (but cook longer) • equal amount brown rice (but cook longer) • equal amount couscous, bulghur or millet
RADICCHIO — See **GREENS, SALAD (spicy)**.		
RADISH	any amount	• equal amount daikon (though it will be hotter)
RAISINS	any amount	*Use one of the following:* • equal amount dried currants, cranberries or cherries • equal amount finely chopped soft prunes, dates or apricots
RAVIOLI — See **PASTA, stuffed**.		

Ingredient Specified	Amount	Substitute
RED PEPPER FLAKES, HOT	any amount	***Use one of the following:*** • equal amount chopped dried red pepper pods • lesser amount red pepper (cayenne) • dash of bottled hot pepper sauce • twice as much chili paste

RED PEPPER SAUCE — See **HOT PEPPER SAUCE**.

RHUBARB, fresh	any amount	• equal amount frozen rhubarb • equal amount cranberries or quince

RICE	any amount	***Use equal amount of substitute:***
• **arborio rice**		• any short- or medium-grain white rice
• **Basmati rice**		• any long-grain white rice
• **specific long-grain white**		• any other long-grain white
• **specific long-grain brown**		• any other long-grain brown
• **any long-grain brown or white**		• any medium-grain or short-grain brown or white (check cooking times)
• **brown**		• wild rice (check cooking times)
• **short- or long-grain brown**		• bulghur (check cooking times)

RICE, WILD — See **WILD RICE**.

Ingredient Specified	Amount	Substitute
RICE FLOUR	any amount	• equal amount cake flour, barley flour or pastry flour
RICE VERMICELLI (Oriental) — See **NOODLES, Oriental.**		
RICE VINEGAR — See **VINEGAR, rice.**		
RIGATONI — See **PASTA, tubes.**		
ROSE WATER	any amount	• equal amount any flower-based water

FOOD FAQs QUICK ANSWER

Virtually all medium- and long-grain rice products are interchangeable in recipes and as side dishes. For the closest match in texture to a specialty rice specified in a recipe, choose another product of equal length grain when possible.

SUBSTITUTIONS

Ingredient Specified	Amount	Substitute
ROSEMARY		
• dried	any amount	*Use one of the following dried herbs, starting with one-half the quantity specified and adding more, as necessary, to taste:* • savory • tarragon • thyme
• fresh	leaves from 4" stem	• ¼ teaspoon dried rosemary
	any amount	• equal amount oregano or sweet basil

ROTELLE — See **PASTA, shapes.**

ROTINI — See **PASTA, shapes.**

RUM — See **LIQUOR.**

RUTABAGA	any amount	*Use one of the following:* • equal amount turnips • equal amount butternut squash

RYE		
• berries	any amount	• equal amount wheat berries
• flakes	any amount	• equal amount rolled oats
• flour	any amount	• equal amount triticale flour

Ingredient Specified	Amount	Substitute
SAFFRON	any amount	• four times as much turmeric
SAGE		
• dried	any amount	*Use one of the following dried herbs, starting with one-half the quantity specified and adding more, as necessary, to taste:* • marjoram • poultry seasoning • rosemary • savory • thyme
• fresh	10 leaves	• ¾ teaspoon dried sage
SALSIFY	any amount	*Use one of the following:* • Black and white salsify are interchangeable in equal amounts. • equal amount parsnip • equal amount artichoke heart • equal amount asparagus
SALT		
• kosher	1 teaspoon	• ½ teaspoon table or sea salt
• sea	1 teaspoon	• 1 teaspoon table salt • 2 teaspoons kosher salt
• table	1 teaspoon	• 1 teaspoon sea salt • 2 teaspoons kosher salt

SUBSTITUTIONS

Ingredient Specified	Amount	Substitute
SAUSAGE		
• andouille (Cajun)	any amount	• equal amount hot smoked pork sausage
• Chinese sausage	any amount	• equal amount any sweet, mild dry sausage
• chorizo, Mexican	any amount	*Use one of the following in equal measure:* • hot Italian sausage • mild Italian sausage • spicy breakfast sausage • Spanish chorizo
• chorizo, Spanish	any amount	*Use one of the following in equal measure:* • Kielbasa • other dry-cured pork sausage • Mexican chorizo
• Kielbasa	any amount	*Use one of the following in equal measure:* • Spanish chorizo • linguica
• linguica	any amount	• equal amount Kielbasa

SCALLION — See ONION, GREEN.

SCALLOPS	any amount	*Use one of the following in equal measure:* • monkfish cubes • shrimp, crab or lobster

Ingredient Specified	Amount	Substitute
SEITAN	any amount	• equal amount tofu
SESAME PASTE, CHINESE	any amount	*Use one of the following in equal measure:* • tahini • peanut butter
SESAME SEEDS	any amount	*Use one of the following in equal measure:* • finely chopped almonds • pumpkin seeds
SHALLOT	any amount	*Use one of the following in equal measure:* • green onions • leeks • onions • scallions
SHERRY — See **WINE, heavy.**		
SHORTENING, VEGETABLE (solid)	any quantity	• $1/3$ less vegetable oil than recipe specifies
• **in baking**	1 cup	• 1 cup + 2 tablespoons butter or margarine • 1 cup minus 2 tablespoons lard • *1 cup applesauce (lower-fat alternative)*

Ingredient Specified	Amount	Substitute
SHRIMP		
• **raw**	12 ounces in shell	• 4½-ounce can of shrimp meat
• **cooked**	3 cups	• 12-ounce package frozen shrimp
	any amount	• equal amount cooked lobster, scallops or crab
SHRIMP PASTE	any amount	• equal amount anchovy paste
SKIM MILK — See **MILK, nonfat.**		
SNAILS, FRESH	1 pound	• 48 canned snails
SOMEN (Japanese) — See **NOODLES, Oriental.**		
SOUR CREAM — See **CREAM, sour.**		
SOUR MILK — See **MILK, sour.**		
SOY SAUCE	¼ cup	• 3 tablespoons Worcestershire sauce + 1 tablespoon water
SPAGHETTI — See **PASTA, rods and ribbons (thin).**		
SPICES	1½ teaspoon whole	• 1 teaspoon ground
	See also specific spices and ***FOOD FAQs* QUICK ANSWER** on page 27.	

Ingredient Specified	Amount	Substitute
SPINACH — See also **GREENS, TANGY (sharp).**		
• **fresh**	I pound	• 10-ounce package frozen spinach • I ½ 10-ounce bags
	any amount	• equal amount Swiss chard
• **frozen**	10-ounce package	• I pound fresh spinach
SQUASH, SUMMER (e.g., chayote, crookneck, pattypan, straightneck, yellow squash, zucchini)	any amount	• All varieties of summer squash are interchangeable in recipes in equal measure.
SQUASH, WINTER	any amount	*Use equal measure, by weight or volume, from among the following substitutes:*
• **acorn**		• golden nugget, butternut or buttercup squash • pumpkin
• **buttercup**		• butternut, acorn or Hubbard squash • pumpkin
• **butternut**		• acorn, buttercup or Hubbard squash
• **golden nugget**		• acorn squash
• **Hubbard**		• pumpkin • butternut, buttercup or acorn squash
• **spaghetti squash**	I medium (5-6 cups cooked)	• 10-12 ounces pasta (rods or ribbons)

SUBSTITUTIONS

Ingredient Specified	Amount	Substitute
STAR ANISE	any amount	*Use one of the following in equal measure:* • anise seed (aniseed) • Chinese five-spice powder
STRUDEL DOUGH	any amount	• equal amount phyllo dough
SUGAR, BROWN • dark	 I cup packed	 *Use one of the following:* • I cup packed light brown sugar + I tablespoon molasses • I cup granulated white sugar • 2 cups sifted powdered sugar • I cup granulated white sugar + ¼ cup light molasses
• light	I cup packed	• ½ cup firmly packed dark brown sugar + ½ cup granulated sugar
SUGAR, POWDERED **(powdered confectioners')**	I cup	*Use one of the following:* • I cup granulated sugar + I tablespoon cornstarch well blended until powdery
• **in cooking and baking**	I cup	• ½ cup + I tablespoon granulated sugar • I ⅓ cups granulated brown sugar

Ingredient Specified	Amount	Substitute
SUGAR, GRANULATED (white)	I cup	*Use one of the following:* • 1¾ cups powdered confectioners sugar, packed • I cup brown sugar, firmly packed • I cup superfine sugar
	I teaspoon	• 2 sugar cubes, ½-inch each • ⅛ teaspoon non-caloric sweetener
	I cube, ½-inch	• ½ teaspoon granulated sugar
• **in baking**	I cup	• ¾ cup honey, corn syrup or maple syrup; reduce liquid in recipe by ¼ cup (never substitute more than ½ of recipe's solid sugar with liquid one) • I cup firmly packed brown sugar or 1⅓ cups granulated brown sugar • 1-1¼ cups molasses + ½ teaspoon baking soda; reduce liquid in recipe by 5 tablespoons (never substitute more than ½ of recipe's solid sugar with liquid one)

SWISS CHARD — See **GREENS, TANGY (sharp).**

SYRUP, CORN — See **CORN SYRUP.**

SYRUP, MAPLE — See **MAPLE SYRUP.**

TABASCO SAUCE	¼ teaspoon	*Use one of the following:* • ⅛-¼ teaspoon red pepper flakes • ¼ teaspoon cayenne

T

Ingredient Specified	Amount	Substitute
TAHINI	any amount	*Use one of the following:* • equal amount Chinese sesame paste • 3 parts peanut butter + 1 part sesame oil • equal amount peanut butter • equal amount ground sesame seeds
TAPIOCA (for thickening)	2 teaspoons	• 1 tablespoon flour
TARRAGON • **dried**	 any amount	 *Use one of the following dried herbs, starting with one-half the quantity specified and adding more, as necessary, to taste:* • marjoram • oregano • rosemary
• **fresh**	any amount	*Use one of the following in equal measure:* • fresh chervil • fresh fennel leaves • fresh basil leaves
TARTAR SAUCE	½ cup	• 6 tablespoons mayonnaise blended with 2 tablespoons minced pickles or pickle relish

Ingredient Specified	Amount	Substitute
THYME		
• dried	any amount	*Use one of the following dried herbs, starting with one-half the quantity specified and adding more, as necessary, to taste:* • basil • marjoram • oregano • savory
• fresh	1 tablespoon of 1 sprig	• 1 teaspoon dried
TOFU	any amount	• any amount seitan
TOMATILLO	1 cup chopped	• 1 cup chopped pickled or fresh green tomatoes
TOMATO		
• fresh		
· **not peeled, seeded**	1 pound	• 3 cups canned tomatoes with juice (2 cans, 14½-16 ounces each, undrained)
· **peeled, seeded**	1 pound	• 2 cups drained canned tomatoes (2 cans, 14½-16 ounces each, drained)
• fresh	1 medium	• 1 cup canned tomatoes, undrained
· **cooked and seasoned**	1 pound	• 8-ounce can of tomato sauce
· **chopped**	1 cup	• ½ cup tomato sauce + ½ cup water
• canned	2 cups	• 2½ cups peeled fresh tomatoes, seasoned and cooked for 10 minutes
• sun-dried	½ cup chopped	• 4-6 fresh plum tomatoes, seeded and chopped (sauce will be saucier) • 1½ cups drained canned tomatoes (sauce will be saucier)

SUBSTITUTIONS

Ingredient Specified	Amount	Substitute
TOMATO JUICE	I cup	*Use one of the following:* • ½ cup tomato sauce + ½ cup water • 2 or 3 fresh ripe tomatoes, peeled, seeded and blended + salt and lemon juice to taste • ¼ cup tomato paste + ¾ cup water + dash of salt and sugar
TOMATO PASTE	I tablespoon	*Use one of the following:* • ½ cup tomato sauce minus ¼-½ cup other liquid in recipe • I tablespoon ketchup
TOMATO PURÉE	I cup	*Use one of the following:* • I cup tomato sauce • ½ cup tomato paste + ½ cup water • 2 cups whole canned tomatoes, drained and puréed
TOMATO SAUCE	I cup	*Use one of the following:* • ³/₈ cup tomato paste + ½ cup water • I cup tomato purée
TOMATO SOUP	10-ounce can	• I cup tomato sauce + ¼ cup water

Ingredient Specified	Amount	Substitute
TRITICALE		
• berries	any amount	• equal amount wheat or rye berries or flakes
• flakes	any amount	• equal amount rolled oats
• flour	any amount	• equal amount whole wheat or rye flour
TURKEY	any amount cooked	• equal amount cooked chicken
TURMERIC, ground	any amount	*Use one of the following in equal measure:* • saffron • mustard powder • curry powder
TURNIP	any amount	*Use an equal amount of one of the following:* • kohlrabi • rutabaga • parsnip • carrot

TURNIP GREENS — See **GREENS, TANGY (bitter)**.

SUBSTITUTIONS

Ingredient Specified	Amount	Substitute
UDON — See **NOODLES, Oriental.**		
VANILLA BEAN	1" piece	• 1 teaspoon pure vanilla extract
VANILLA EXTRACT	any amount	• equal amount almond extract
VEAL	1 cutlet	*Use one of the following:* • 1 turkey cutlet • 1 chicken cutlet • 1 pork cutlet

FOOD FAQs QUICK ANSWER

Various types of venison, the edible meat of game animals such as deer, elk and moose, can be used interchangeably in recipes and meal planning. For a less "gamy" substitute, use beef.

Ingredient Specified	Amount	Substitute
VEGETABLES — See also specific vegetables.		
• **canned**	I pound drained	***Use one of the following:***
		• 2 cups cut-up fresh vegetables, cooked
		• 2 cups frozen loose-pack vegetables, cooked and drained
• **frozen**	I0-ounce package	***Use one of the following:***
		• 2 cups cut-up fresh vegetables
		• 2 cups canned vegetables, drained

VEGETABLE OIL — See **OIL, vegetable**.

VERMICELLI — See **PASTA, rods and ribbons (thin)**.

VERMOUTH	any amount	• equal amount dry white wine or dry sherry

SUBSTITUTIONS

Ingredient Specified	Amount	Substitute
VINEGAR	1 teaspoon	***Use one of the following:*** • 2 teaspoons lemon juice • 2 teaspoons wine (in marinades)
		Substitute freely among choices in each of the following groups:
• **Balsamic vinegar**	any amount	• equal amount sherry vinegar • equal amount red wine vinegar
• **cider vinegar**	any amount	• equal amount malt vinegar • equal amount rice vinegar • equal amount wine vinegar
• **malt vinegar**	any amount	• equal amount cider vinegar • equal amount wine vinegar
• **red wine vinegar**	any amount	• equal amount white wine vinegar • equal amount Balsamic vinegar • equal amount sherry vinegar • small amount of red wine + cider vinegar to equal amount specified
• **rice vinegar**	½ cup	• ⅓ cup white (distilled) vinegar + 3 tablespoons water • ½ cup cider vinegar
• **sherry vinegar**	any amount	• equal amount Balsamic vinegar • equal amount red wine vinegar
• **white wine vinegar**	any amount	• equal amount red wine vinegar • equal amount rice vinegar • equal amount cider vinegar • small amount of white wine + white distilled vinegar to equal amount specified

Ingredient Specified	Amount	Substitute

WALNUTS — See also NUTS.

| | any amount | • equal amount pecans |

WASABI | any amount | *Use one of the following:*
• hot mustard powder mixed with small amount of water to equal amount specified in paste form
• equal amount horseradish

WATER CHESTNUT

| • canned slices | any amount | *Use one of the following in equal measure:*
• sliced jicama
• Jerusalem artichoke |
| • fresh | 15-17 water chestnuts | • 5-ounce can water chestnuts |

WATERCRESS — See GREENS, SALAD (spicy).

WHEAT

• berries	any amount	• equal amount of any groat or grain berry (though cooking times may vary)
• bran	any amount	• equal amount oat bran or wheat germ
• bulghur	any amount	• equal amount cracked wheat
• flakes	any amount	• equal amount of any grain flake
• germ	any amount	• equal amount wheat bran

SUBSTITUTIONS

Ingredient Specified	Amount	Substitute
WHISKEY — See **LIQUOR**.		
WILD RICE	any amount	*Use one of the following:* • equal amount Wehani brown rice • equal amount long-grain white rice
WINE (in recipes), **red or white**	any amount	*Use one of the following in equal measure:* • fish, chicken, beef or vegetable broth • water
• red	any amount	• equal measure unsweetened grape juice or cranberry juice
• white	any amount	*Use one of the following in equal measure:* • apple or white grape juice • dry white vermouth or dry sherry
WINE (in recipes), heavy **(e.g., Madeira, Marsala,** **port and sherry)**	2 tablespoons	*Use one of the following:* • Madeira, Marsala, port and sherry can be used interchangeably in equal amounts. • ½ cup dry red or white wine
WINE (in recipes), rice	any amount	• equal amount dry sherry, sake or gin
• mirin (Japanese **rice wine)**	any amount	• equal amount sweet sherry or sweet vermouth
• sake	any amount	• equal amount dry sherry, dry vermouth or Chinese rice wine

Ingredient Specified	Amount	Substitute
WINE (for marinade)	½ cup	*Use one of the following:* • ¼ cup vinegar + 1 tablespoon sugar + ¼ cup water • 1 tablespoon vinegar + chicken stock or water to fill ½ cup
WINTER SQUASH — See **SQUASH, WINTER.**		
WONTON WRAPPERS	any number	• egg roll wrappers cut into quarters to equal same number
WORCESTERSHIRE SAUCE	1 tablespoon	*Use one of the following:* • 1 tablespoon light soy sauce + dash of hot pepper • 1 tablespoon soy sauce + dash of garlic powder and cayenne pepper • 1 tablespoon steak sauce
YEAST • **active dry**	1 envelope (¼ ounce)	*Use one of the following:* • 1 standard cake (³/₅ ounce) of compressed yeast • 1 tablespoon fast-rising active yeast • 1 tablespoon loose yeast
• **compressed**	1 cake (³/₅ ounce)	• 1 package or 1 tablespoon active dry yeast

Y

Ingredient Specified	Amount	Substitute
YOGURT, plain	any amount	***Use one of the following in equal measure:*** • buttermilk • sour cream • heavy cream • mayonnaise • cottage cheese, blended until smooth • *lowfat or nonfat yogurt (lower-fat alternative)*

Z

ZEST OF FRUIT	I teaspoon freshly grated	***Use one of the following:*** • I teaspoon dried zest of fruit • ½ teaspoon extract of fruit • 2 tablespoons fresh juice of fruit • 2 teaspoons grated candied peel of fruit

ZITI — See **PASTA, tubes.**

Yields & Equivalents

Dairy Products

	BEFORE Preparation		AFTER Preparation
	Volume	Weight	Approximate Yield
BUTTER			
• **stick**	4 sticks	1 pound	• 2 cups solid or melted
	1 stick	¼ pound	• ½ cup solid or melted
	½ stick	2 ounces	• ¼ cup or 4 tablespoons solid or melted
	¼ stick	1 ounce	• 2 tablespoons solid or melted
	⅛ stick	½ ounce	• 1 tablespoon solid or melted
• **whipped**	1 container	8 ounces	• 25 tablespoons (1½ cups + 1 tablespoon)
CHEESE			
• **firm (e.g., cheddar, colby, gruyère, jack, Jarlsberg, Muenster, string, Swiss)**	1½" chunk	2 ounces	• ½ cup grated, lightly packed
• **hard (e.g., asiago, fontina, Parmesan, Romano)**	1½" chunk	2 ounces	• ½ cup grated, lightly packed
• **processed (e.g., American)**	2½-3 slices; or ½" slice of cheese loaf	2 ounces	• ½ cup shredded, lightly packed
• **semisoft (e.g., blue, feta, Gorgonzola, mozzarella, Roquefort, Stilton)**	1½" chunk	2 ounces	• ½ cup crumbled, lightly packed

Dairy Products

	BEFORE Preparation		AFTER Preparation
	Volume	**Weight**	**Approximate Yield**
CHEESE, *continued*			
• soft			
· cottage cheese, farmers, ricotta	I container	8 ounces	• I cup
· cream cheese			
- brick	I loaf	8 ounces	• 16 tablespoons or I cup
- tub, regular	I container	8 ounces	• 16 tablespoons or I cup
- fat-free or reduced fat	I container	8 ounces	• 14 tablespoons
· goat (e.g., chevré)	I ¼" cube	2 ounces	• ¼ cup crumbled, lightly packed
CREAM			
• heavy (or heavy whipping)	I cup	8 ounces	• 2 cups whipped
• sour	I container	8 ounces	• I cup
• whipping (or light whipping)	I cup	8 ounces	• 2 cups whipped
EGG			
• large	I raw egg		• 3 tablespoons whites and yolks
	I hard-cooked		• ¹/₃ cup finely chopped
	I dozen	24 ounces	• 4 eggs per cup, whites and yolks
• medium	I dozen	21 ounces	• 5 eggs per cup, whites and yolks
• small	I dozen	18 ounces	• 6 eggs per cup, whites and yolks

| | BEFORE Preparation | | AFTER Preparation |
	Volume	Weight	Approximate Yield
EGG WHITE	1 large		• 2 tablespoons white; *or* ¾ cup whites beaten to stiff peaks
	4 large		• ½ cup whites; *or* 3 cups whites beaten to stiff peaks
EGG YOLK	1 large		• 1 tablespoon yolk
	7-8 large		• ½ cup yolks
MARGARINE — See **Fats and Oils** section.			

When stiffly beaten, egg whites will expand to approximately 6 times their unwhipped volume. But they will not whip up if even a speck of yolk is included or if the dishes or utensils used for whipping have any oil or fat on them.

YIELDS & EQUIVALENTS

| | BEFORE Preparation | | AFTER Preparation |
	Volume	Weight	Approximate Yield
MILK			
• **condensed**	1 can	14 ounces	• 1²/₃ cups
• **dry or powdered (nonfat, whole, buttermilk)**	4 tablespoons	less than 1 ounce	• 1 cup reconstituted
• **evaporated**	12-ounce can		• 1½ cups; *or* 3 cups reconstituted
• **whole; nonfat; buttermilk**	1 quart		• 4 cups
YOGURT	1 container	16 ounces	• 2 cups; *or* 1 cup yogurt cheese (drained 4 hours)

FOOD FAQs QUICK ANSWER

Unless otherwise noted, recipes calling for "eggs" anticipate the use of large eggs.

| | BEFORE Preparation | | AFTER Preparation |
	Volume	Weight	Approximate Yield
BUTTER			
• stick	4 sticks	I pound	• 2 cups solid or melted
	I stick	¼ pound	• ½ cup solid or melted
	½ stick	2 ounces	• ¼ cup or 4 tablespoons solid or melted
	¼ stick	I ounce	• 2 tablespoons solid or melted
	⅛ stick	½ ounce	• I tablespoon solid or melted
• whipped	I container	8 ounces	• 25 tablespoons (1½ cups + I tablespoon)
COOKING OIL — See OIL, cooking.			
LARD	2 cups	I pound	
MARGARINE			
• stick	4 sticks	I pound	• 2 cups solid or melted
	I stick	¼ pound	• ½ cup solid or melted
	½ stick	2 ounces	• ¼ cup or 4 tablespoons solid or melted
	¼ stick	I ounce	• 2 tablespoons solid or melted
	⅛ stick	½ ounce	• I tablespoon solid or melted
• tub	I container	8 ounces	• 16 tablespoons

YIELDS & EQUIVALENTS

	BEFORE Preparation Volume	Weight	AFTER Preparation Approximate Yield
OIL			
• cooking	16 ounces		• 2 cups
• vegetable	16 ounces		• 2 cups
SHORTENING — See **VEGETABLE SHORTENING**.			
VEGETABLE OIL — See **OIL, vegetable**.			
VEGETABLE SHORTENING	2⅓ cups	1 pound	

| | BEFORE Preparation | | AFTER Preparation |
	Volume	Weight	Approximate Yield
APPLE			
• fresh	1 medium	$1/3$ pound	• 1 cup diced, sliced or chopped
	2 large *or* 3 medium *or* 4 small	1 pound	• 3 cups diced, sliced or chopped
• dried chunks	1 package	6 ounces	• 2 cups chunks or chopped
APRICOT			
• fresh	8-12 medium	1 pound	• $2^1/2$-$2^2/3$ cups diced or sliced; *or* $1^1/2$-2 cups mashed
• dried	1 package	6 ounces	• 2 cups halves; *or* $3/4$ cup finely chopped
AVOCADO	1 small	5-7 ounces	• $3/4$-1 cup diced; *or* $1/2$-$5/8$ cup mashed
	1 medium	7-9 ounces	• 1-$1^1/4$ cups diced; *or* $5/8$-$3/4$ cup mashed
BANANA			
• fresh	1 medium	$1/3$ pound	• $1/2$ cup mashed
	2 large *or* 3 medium *or* 4 small	1 pound	• $1^1/2$ cup mashed; *or* 2 cups sliced
• dried	1 package	8 ounces	• $1^1/2$ cups sliced

YIELDS & EQUIVALENTS

	BEFORE Preparation		AFTER Preparation
	Volume	**Weight**	**Approximate Yield**

BERRIES — See **BLACKBERRIES, BLUEBERRIES, RASPBERRIES** and **STRAWBERRIES.**

	BEFORE Preparation Volume	Weight	AFTER Preparation Approximate Yield
BLACKBERRIES	I small container	6 ounces	• I cup
BLUEBERRIES			
• fresh	I small container	6 ounces	• I cup
• frozen	I package	I pound	• 2¼ cups
CANTALOUPE	I small	2-2½ pounds	• 2½-3¼ cups cubed or diced
	I medium	2½-3 pounds	• 3¼-4 cups cubed or diced
	I large	3+ pounds	• 4 or more cups cubed or diced
CHERIMOYA	I large	I pound	• 2 cups cubed, peeled and seeded; *or* I½ cups mashed
CHERRIES			
• whole fresh	3 cups	I pound	• 2½ cups pitted and halved
• dried	I package	6 ounces	• I cup

	BEFORE Preparation		AFTER Preparation
	Volume	**Weight**	**Approximate Yield**
COCONUT			
• **dried**	1 package	4 ounces	• 1 1/3 cups, loosely packed
• **flaked or shredded**	1 package	14 ounces	• 5 cups, loosely packed
• **fresh**	1 medium	1 1/2-1 3/4 pounds	• 3-3 1/2 cups grated, loosely packed; *or* 3/8 cup juice
CRANBERRIES			
• **fresh or frozen**	1 package	12 ounces	• 3 cups whole berries
• **dried**	1 package	6 ounces	• 1 3/4 cups whole berries

FOOD FAQs QUICK ANSWER

To get approximately ½ cup of fruit purée, use 4 ounces of *fresh* berries or juicy fruit *or* 1 cup of *cooked and drained* berries or juicy fruit.

YIELDS & EQUIVALENTS

	BEFORE Preparation Volume	Weight	AFTER Preparation Approximate Yield
CURRANTS, dried	1 package	10 ounces	• 1¾ cups
DATES			
• **fresh**			
· **with pits**	16-18 small	4 ounces	• ⅔ cup pitted and chopped
· **pitted**	20-24 small	4 ounces	• ¾ cup chopped
• **dried**			
· **with pits**	32-36 small	8 ounces	• 1⅓ cups pitted and chopped
· **pitted**	1 package	8 ounces	• 1½ cups chopped
DRIED FRUIT — See specific fruits.			
FEIJOA	8-10 large	1½-2 pounds	• 1 cup pulp
FIGS			
• **fresh**	6-8 large or 12-16 small	1 pound	• 4 cups sliced; *or* 3 cups chopped
• **dried**	1 package	8 ounces	• 1½ cups chopped
GRAPEFRUIT	1 medium	12-14 ounces	• 1-1¼ cups segments; *or* 1 cup juice

	BEFORE Preparation Volume	Weight	AFTER Preparation Approximate Yield
GRAPES	2½-3 cups	I pound	• 2½-3 cups halved
HONEYDEW MELON — See **MELON**.			
KIWI	I average (2" oval)	3 ounces	• ⅓-½ cup sliced
	5-6 average	I pound	• 2 cups mashed
KUMQUATS	10 average	¼ pound	
LEMON	I medium	4 ounces	• 3 tablespoons juice; *or* 2-3 tablespoons grated rind; *or* 2-3 teaspoons grated zest
	4 medium	I pound	• ¾ cup juice; *or* ½-¾ cup grated rind; *or* 3-4 tablespoons grated zest
LIME	I medium	2½-3 ounces	• 1½-2 tablespoons juice; *or* I tablespoon grated rind; *or* ½-I teaspoon grated zest
	6 medium	I pound	• ½-¾ cup juice; *or* ⅜ cup grated rind; *or* 1-2 tablespoons grated zest

YIELDS & EQUIVALENTS

	BEFORE Preparation Volume	Weight	AFTER Preparation Approximate Yield
MANGO	I small	10 ounces	• ¾ cup chopped; *or* ½ cup puréed
MELON	Varies by type	I pound with rind and seeds	• 1½ cups cubed fruit
NECTARINE	3 medium *or* 4 small	I pound	• 2-2½ cups sliced or chopped
OLIVES — See **Miscellaneous** section.			
ORANGE	I medium	⅓ pound	• ⅓ cup juice; *or* ¼ cup grated rind; *or* 2 tablespoons grated zest
	3 medium or 2 large	I pound	• I cup juice; *or* ¾ cup grated rind; *or* ³⁄₈ cup grated zest
PAPAYA	I medium	I pound	• 1¼-1½ cups peeled and seeded, sliced or cubed; *or* ¾-1 cup mashed
PASSION FRUIT	I average (2" long) 10-12 average	2-3 ounces 1-1½ pounds	• 4-6 teaspoons pulp and seeds • I cup pulp and seeds or purée

	BEFORE Preparation		AFTER Preparation
	Volume	**Weight**	**Approximate Yield**
PEACH			
• fresh	1 medium	1/3 pound	• ¾ cup cubed, chopped or sliced; *or* 1/3 -1/2 cup mashed
	3 medium *or* 2 large	1 pound	• 2-2¼ cups peeled and cubed, chopped or sliced; *or* 1-1 1/3 cups mashed
• dried	1 package	7 ounces	• 1½ cups
• canned	1 can	16 ounces	• 1¾ cups fruit with syrup

FOOD FAQs QUICK ANSWER

A 16-20 ounce can of fruit will yield 1¾-2 cups of drained fruit. A 10-ounce package of frozen fruit will yield approximately 1¼ cups of fruit.

YIELDS & EQUIVALENTS

	BEFORE Preparation		AFTER Preparation
	Volume	Weight	Approximate Yield
PEAR			
• fresh	1 medium	1/3 pound	• 3/4 cup diced, chopped or sliced
	3 medium *or* 4 small	1 pound	• 2-2 1/2 cups sliced or diced
• dried	1 package	7 ounces	• 1 2/3 cups
• canned	1 can	16 ounces	• 1 3/4 cups fruit with syrup
PEPINO	1 (3-3 1/2" long)	4 ounces	• 1/2 cup peeled and sliced; *or* 1/3 cup pulp
PERSIMMON	1 Hachiya or other soft variety	7-8 ounces	• 1/2 cup pulp; *or* 1/3-1/2 cup purée
	1 crisp variety	5-6 ounces	• 3/4-1 cup sliced
PINEAPPLE			
• fresh	1 medium	3-3 1/2 pounds	• 1 3/4 pounds peeled, trimmed and cored; *or* 3 1/2-4 cups sliced or cubed
• canned chunks or crushed	1 can	20 ounces	• 2 1/2 cups fruit and syrup; *or* 2 cups fruit, drained

	BEFORE Preparation Volume	Weight	AFTER Preparation Approximate Yield
PLANTAIN	2 large *or* 3 medium	I pound	• I cup mashed; *or* 2 cups sliced
PLUMS			
• **Japanese varieties**	6 average (each 2" diameter)	I pound	• 2½-3 cups sliced or chopped
• **European varieties**	12-15 average	I pound	• 2 cups sliced
POMEGRANATE	I medium	7 ounces	• ¾ cup seeds; *or* ½ cup juice
PRICKLY PEAR	I medium	3-4 ounces	• ¼-⅓ cup sliced or cubed
PRUNES, dried			
• **with pits**	52 medium	12 ounces	• 1¾ cups pitted and chopped
• **without pits**	I package	12 ounces	• 2 cups chopped
PUMPKIN			
• **fresh**	I medium	5 pounds	• 4½ cups cooked and mashed fruit
• **canned**	I can	16 ounces	• 2 cups mashed fruit

YIELDS & EQUIVALENTS

	BEFORE Preparation Volume	Weight	AFTER Preparation Approximate Yield
QUINCE	3 large	1 pound	• 1½ cups pulp; or 2 cups juice
RAISINS	3 cups, loosely packed	1 pound	• 2½ cups firmly packed
RASPBERRIES	1 small container	6 ounces	• 1 cup
RHUBARB	Stalks: 3-4 large or 4-5 medium or 6-8 small	1 pound	• 3 cups sliced or in 1" chunks; or 2 cups chopped and cooked
SAPOTE	1 medium	7 ounces	• ¾ cup cubed, peeled and seeded
STRAWBERRIES	1 container	12 ounces	• 2 cups, hulled and sliced
TANGERINE	1 average 4 average	¼ pound 1 pound	• ½ cup sections • 2 cups sections
WATERMELON	Varies widely	1 pound with rind	• 1½ cups cubed

Grains and Grain Products

	BEFORE Preparation Volume	Weight	AFTER Preparation Approximate Yield
BARLEY			
• pearl	1 cup	8 ounces	• 4 cups cooked
• quick-cook	1 cup	5 ounces	• 3 cups cooked
BREAD	1 loaf	1 pound	
	14-20 slices	1 pound	
	1 slice	1 ounce	• 1/4-1/3 cup fine dry crumbs
			• 1/2-3/4 cup soft crumbs
BREADCRUMBS — See also **COOKIE CRUMBS** and **CRACKER CRUMBS**.			
• bread, dry	1 slice	1 ounce	• 1/4-1/3 cup fine dry crumbs
• bread, fresh	1 slice	1 ounce	• 1/2-3/4 cup soft crumbs
• cornbread	4 1/2" square		• 1 cup crumbs
BUCKWHEAT GROATS	1 cup	6 1/2 ounces	• 3 1/2-4 cups cooked
CEREAL CRUMBS	3 cups flakes		• 1 cup crushed crumbs

Grains and Grain Products

	BEFORE Preparation		AFTER Preparation
	Volume	**Weight**	**Approximate Yield**
COOKIE CRUMBS			
• chocolate wafers	19 cookies	4 ounces	• I cup finely crushed crumbs
• gingersnaps	15 cookies	3¾-4 ounces	• I cup finely crushed crumbs
• Oreos with filling	14 cookies	5½ ounces	• I cup finely crushed crumbs
• shortbread	17 cookies	4½ ounces	• I cup finely crushed crumbs
• vanilla wafers	22 cookies	3-3¼ ounces	• I cup finely crushed crumbs
CORNMEAL	I cup	6 ounces	• 3½-4 cups cooked
CORNSTARCH	3 cups	I pound	
CRACKER CRUMBS			
• graham	14 squares	3½-4 ounces	• I cup finely crushed crumbs
	9 squares	2½ ounces	• I cup coarsely crushed crumbs
• matzoh	6 sheets	5½-6 ounces	• I cup finely crushed crumbs
• rich, round	24 crackers	2½-3 ounces	• I cup finely crushed crumbs
• saltine	28 crackers	2¾-3 ounces	• I cup finely crushed crumbs

	BEFORE Preparation Volume	Weight	AFTER Preparation Approximate Yield
FLOUR			
• all-purpose (pre-sifted)	3½ cups	1 pound	• 4 cups if sifted
• bread	3½ cups	1 pound	• 3⅔ cups if sifted
• cake	4 cups	1 pound	• 4½ cups if sifted
• graham	3½ cups	1 pound	• 3¾ cups if sifted
• rye (medium grain)	4 ½ cups	1 pound	• 4¾ cups if sifted
• whole wheat	3½ cups	1 pound	• 4 cups if sifted
HOMINY GRITS			
• quick-cooking	¼ cup	1½ ounces	• 1 cup cooked
KASHA	1 cup	6½ ounces	• 3½-4 cups cooked
MILLET	1 cup	8 ounces	• 3½ cups cooked
OATS			
• bran	⅓ cup	1 ounce	
• rolled oats			
· quick-cooking	½ cup	2 ounces	• ¾ cup cooked
· regular (old-fashioned)	½ cup	2 ounces	• ¾-1 cup cooked
• steel cut oats	½ cup	2 ounces	• 1¼ cups cooked

YIELDS & EQUIVALENTS

	BEFORE Preparation Volume	Weight	AFTER Preparation Approximate Yield
PHYLLO DOUGH PASTRY LEAVES	l package	l pound	• 25 sheets
POPCORN	¼ cup kernels	2 ounces	• 5-6 cups popped
QUINOA	l cup	6 ounces	• 3½ cups cooked

FOOD FAQs QUICK ANSWER

Most grains expand to 2 to 4 times their original size when cooked. Factors that will affect the yield include the amount of water used and the length of time the grain is cooked.

| | BEFORE Preparation | | AFTER Preparation |
	Volume	Weight	Approximate Yield
RICE, aromatic			
• **Basmati**	1 cup	6 ounces	• 3 cups cooked
• **Texmati**	1 cup	6½ ounces	• 3 cups cooked
RICE, brown			
• **long-grain**	1 cup	7 ounces	• 3 cups cooked
• **short-grain**	1 cup	7 ounces	• 3 cups cooked
• **converted (parboiled)**	1 cup	7 ounces	• 3⅓ cups cooked
RICE, white			
• **long-grain**	1 cup	7 ounces	• 3 cups cooked
• **medium-grain**	1 cup	8 ounces	• 3 cups cooked
• **short-grain**	1 cup	7 ounces	• 3 cups cooked
• **converted (parboiled)**	1 cup	7 ounces	• 4 cups cooked
• **quick-cooking**	1 cup	3 ounces	• 2 cups cooked
RICE, wild — See **WILD RICE**.			
RYE			
• **berries**	1 cup	7 ounces	• 3 cups cooked

Grains and Grain Products

YIELDS & EQUIVALENTS

	BEFORE Preparation		AFTER Preparation
	Volume	Weight	Approximate Yield
WHEAT — See also **FLOUR**.			
• **berries**	1 cup	7½ ounces	• 2½ cups cooked
• **bran**	¼ cup	½ ounce	
• **bulghur**	1 cup	6 ounces	• 3 cups cooked
• **germ**	3 tablespoons	1 ounce	
WILD RICE	1 cup	5½ ounces	• 3½-4 cups cooked
WONTON WRAPPERS	1 package	14-16 ounces	• about 60 wrappers

	BEFORE Preparation		AFTER Preparation
	Volume	Weight	Approximate Yield
ALLSPICE	5 whole berries		• I teaspoon ground
ANISE SEED (aniseed)	I teaspoon seed		• I teaspoon ground
BASIL	I average bunch	2½-3 ounces	• 2-2¼ cups whole leaves, loosely packed; *or* 1½ cups leaves, sliced; *or* ⅓ cup leaves finely chopped
BAY LEAF	I whole leaf		• ¼ teaspoon crumbled; *or* ⅛ teaspoon ground

FOOD FAQs QUICK ANSWER

Many spices, such as annatto, caraway, celery, poppy and sesame seeds, are extremely small in their natural forms and, therefore, are rarely used in any other form.

Herbs and Spices

	BEFORE Preparation Volume	Weight	AFTER Preparation Approximate Yield
CAPERS	I bottle	4 ounces	• 5 tablespoons, drained
CARDAMOM PODS	4 medium *or* 8 small		• ½ teaspoon ground
CHIVES	I average bunch	I ounce	• 2 tablespoons snipped chives
CILANTRO (leaf) — See **CORIANDER** for seed.			
	I average bunch	4 ounces, leaves and stems	• 2 cups whole leaves; *or* ⅓ cup finely chopped leaves
CINNAMON	3½" long stick		• I teaspoon ground
CLOVES	I teaspoon whole		• ¾ teaspoon ground
CORIANDER (seed) — See **CILANTRO** for leaf.			
	I teaspoon seeds		• I teaspoon ground
CUMIN	I teaspoon seeds		• I teaspoon ground

	BEFORE Preparation		AFTER Preparation
	Volume	Weight	Approximate Yield
DILL			
• leaf	I large bunch	4 ounces	• I ¼ cups snipped leaves, loosely packed
FENNEL (also called **ANISE**)			
• leaf	Full leaves from 8 ounce bulb		• 3-4 tablespoons snipped leaves
GINGERROOT — See **Vegetables** section.			
HORSERADISH — See **Vegetables** section.			

When freshly ground, some spices may measure more than the original volume used. Once the air settles out of the ground version, it should equal the original volume.

YIELDS & EQUIVALENTS

	BEFORE Preparation Volume	Weight	AFTER Preparation Approximate Yield
LEMONGRASS	1 stalk	¾ ounce	• 1-1½ teaspoon finely chopped bulblike center
MARJORAM	1 average bunch	1 ounce	• 1 cup whole leaves; *or* 5 tablespoons chopped leaves
MINT	1 bunch	1½ ounces	• 1 cup whole leaves; *or* 3 tablespoons minced leaves

FOOD FAQs QUICK ANSWER

Many herbs are available not only in fresh form, but dried and crushed as well. Some, such as thyme and rosemary, are also ground. Still others, such as chives, can be found fresh frozen. Herb flavors are most concentrated in ground form.

	BEFORE Preparation		AFTER Preparation
	Volume	**Weight**	**Approximate Yield**
MUSTARD — See also **MUSTARD, prepared** in **Miscellaneous** section.			
	1 teaspoon seeds		• 1½ teaspoons ground
NUTMEG	1 small pod		• 1 teaspoon ground
OREGANO	1 average bunch	1 ounce	• 1 cup leaves; *or* 5 tablespoons chopped
PARSLEY			
• curly leaf	1 average bunch	5 ounces	• 3½ cups whole leaves; *or* 1½-1¾ cups finely chopped
• Italian	1 average bunch	5-6 ounces	• 3 cups whole leaves; *or* ¾-1 cup finely chopped
PEPPER, hot dried — See also **CHILI PEPPER** in **Vegetables** section.			
	1 small pepper, about 2" long		• ¼ teaspoon crushed or ground flakes
PEPPERCORNS	1 tablespoon whole		• 4 teaspoons finely ground
ROSEMARY	1 average bunch	1 ounce	• 2 tablespoons chopped leaves

Herbs and Spices

| | BEFORE Preparation | | AFTER Preparation |
	Volume	Weight	Approximate Yield
TARRAGON	I average bunch	I ounce	• 2 tablespoons chopped leaves
THYME	I average bunch	I ounce	• ¼ cup leaves; *or* 2 tablespoons chopped

FOOD FAQs QUICK ANSWER

Many common kitchen seasonings, such as chili powder, garlic salt, apple pie spice and pumpkin pie spice, are combinations of herbs, spices and vegetables that are packaged and sold in the combined form.

	BEFORE Preparation		AFTER Preparation
	Volume	**Weight**	**Approximate Yield**

MEAT (e.g., beef, ham, lamb, pork, veal, venison, etc.)

	Volume	Weight	Approximate Yield
• boneless steaks, chops, cutlets, etc.			
· raw		½ pound	• 1 cup ground raw meat; *or* 1 cup cooked and chopped meat
· cooked		½ pound	• 1½ cups chopped
• bacon	16-20 regular *or* 10-14 thick slices	1 pound	• 1½ cups cooked and diced
	4-5 regular slices *or* 2 thick slices	2 ounces	• ¼ cup cooked and diced
• sausage	1 link or patty	varies	• varies

POULTRY — See also *FOOD FAQs* **QUICK ANSWER** on following page.

	Volume	Weight	Approximate Yield
• chicken, broiler/fryer	1 whole	per pound	• 1 cup cooked and diced meat
· breast, skinless & boneless	2 medium breast halves	½ pound	• 1 cup ground raw meat; *or* 1 cup cooked and diced
• turkey	whole	per pound	• 1 cup cooked and diced meat
· breast, skinless & boneless	1 half	2 pounds	• 4 cups cooked and diced meat

Meat, Poultry, Fish and Shellfish

Meat, Poultry, Fish and Shellfish

	BEFORE Preparation		AFTER Preparation
	Volume	**Weight**	**Approximate Yield**
FISH			
• **canned**			
· **anchovy**	I can	2 ounces	• 10-12 fillets
- **anchovy paste**	I tube	1.6 ounces	• 3 tablespoons
· **salmon**	I can	14¾ ounces	• 1¾ cups meat
· **sardines**	I can	3¾ ounces	• 9-10 fish; *or* ½ cup fish, drained, boned and flaked
· **tuna**	I can	9 ounces	• I cup meat, drained

FOOD FAQs QUICK ANSWER

As a general rule, recipes calling for game birds or specialty poultry species, such as duck, goose, Cornish hens, squab, etc., will specify a number of birds or the specific size of the bird to be purchased. Most of these products contain a significantly higher percentage of fat and bone than do chicken and turkey.

	BEFORE Preparation Volume	Weight	AFTER Preparation Approximate Yield

FISH, *continued*
- **whole (fresh or frozen)** — See also *FOOD FAQs* **QUICK ANSWER** below.

· **flatfish (e.g., flounder and sole)**	1 fish	varies	• approximately $1/3$ total weight is edible
· **roundfish (e.g., catfish, cod, snapper, etc.)**	1 fish	varies	• approximately $1/2$ total weight is edible

FOOD FAQs QUICK ANSWER

Many fresh fish, such as Chilean sea bass, some cods, drum, haddock, halibut, jacks, kingclip, mahi-mahi, monkfish, opah, orange roughy, pollocks, rockfish, salmon, shark, skate, sturgeon, swordfish, tuna, whiting and wolffish, are rarely, if ever, available in market as whole fish. They are most frequently found as fillets, steaks or chops of varying weights and sizes.

Meat, Poultry, Fish and Shellfish

YIELDS & EQUIVALENTS

	BEFORE Preparation Volume	Weight	AFTER Preparation Approximate Yield
SHELLFISH, crustaceans			
• **crab** — See also *FOOD FAQs* **QUICK ANSWER** below.			
· **cooked crab meat**		1 pound	• 2 cups meat
	1 can	6 ounces	• 4¼ ounces drained; *or* ⁵⁄₆ cup meat
• **crayfish**	40-50 whole	3-4 pounds	• 2 cups cooked tail meat

FOOD FAQs QUICK ANSWER

The yield of edible meat from commercially available crabs varies according to the type of crab. As a general rule, you can expect to yield 1 pound (or 2-2½ cups) of cooked crab meat from 4 pounds of crab in the shell.

For lobsters, you can expect that 25% of the lobster's weight will be edible after cooking, cracking and picking.

	BEFORE Preparation Volume	Weight	AFTER Preparation Approximate Yield
SHELLFISH, crustaceans, *continued*			
• **lobster** — See also *FOOD FAQs* **QUICK ANSWER** on previous page.			
· **American**	I average	I-I½ pounds	• ¾-I cup cooked meat
· **spiny**		I½ pounds tails	• I-I½ cups cooked meat
• **shrimp**	depends on size	I pound in shell	• I⅓ cups (½ pound) cooked meat
	I can	4¼ ounces, drained	• ½ cup meat
SHELLFISH, mollusks			
• **clams**	2-3 dozen, depending on size		• I½-2 cups minced clam meat
	I can	6½ ounces	• ⅞ cup minced clam meat
• **mussels**	12 average	I pound in shell	• ⅔ cup meat
• **oysters**	12 average in shell		• I cup shucked meat
	I jar	10 ounces	• 16 small oysters; *or* 6-8 medium oysters
• **scallops**			
· **bay**	100	I pound	• 2 cups scallops
· **sea**	30	I pound	• 2 cups scallops

Meat, Poultry, Fish and Shellfish

YIELDS & EQUIVALENTS

	BEFORE Preparation		AFTER Preparation
	Volume	Weight	Approximate Yield
SHELLFISH, mollusks, *continued*			
• squid	2 cups cleaned and sliced	I pound	• 1¼ cups cooked

	BEFORE Preparation		AFTER Preparation
	Volume	Weight	Approximate Yield
ALMONDS			
• in the shell	5 cups (140 nuts)	I pound	• I ¼ cups (6 ounces) shelled whole nuts
• shelled		5 ounces	• I cup nuts
• ground		4 ounces	• ¾ cup, lightly packed
BRAZIL NUTS			
• in the shell	4 cups (50 nuts)	I pound	• I ½ cups (8 ounces) shelled whole nuts
• shelled		5 ⅓ ounces	• I cup whole nuts
CASHEW NUTS			
• shelled	250 nuts	I pound	• 3 ¼ cups whole nuts
		4 ¾ ounces	• I cup whole nuts
CHESTNUTS			
• in the shell	35-40 nuts	I pound	• 2 ½ cups (12 ounces) shelled nuts, *or* 2 cups puréed
• shelled		4 ¾ ounces	• I cup whole nuts

	BEFORE Preparation		AFTER Preparation
	Volume	**Weight**	**Approximate Yield**
HAZELNUTS/FILBERTS			
• in the shell	4 cups (140 nuts)	1 pound	• 1¼ cups (6 ounces) shelled nuts
• shelled		4¾ ounces	• 1 cup nuts
• ground		4 ounces	• ¾ cup, lightly packed
MACADAMIA NUTS			
• in the shell	4½ cups (88 nuts)	1 pound	• 1½ cups (7 ounces) shelled nuts
		4½ ounces	• 1 cup nuts
PEANUTS			
• in the shell	6 cups	1 pound	• 2-2½ cups (11 ounces) shelled nuts
• shelled		4-5 ounces	• 1 cup nuts
	2 cups	8 ounces	• 1 cup peanut butter
PECANS			
• in the shell	4 cups (66 nuts)	1 pound	• 2 cups (7 ounces) shelled nuts
• shelled		3½ ounces	• 1 cup nut halves
PINE NUTS		2½ ounces	• ½ cup

| | BEFORE Preparation | | AFTER Preparation |
	Volume	Weight	Approximate Yield
PISTACHIO NUTS			
• in the shell	4 cups	1 pound	• 2 cups (8 ounces) shelled nuts
• shelled		4 ounces	• 1 cup nuts
WALNUTS			
• in the shell	36 nuts	1 pound	• 2 cups (8 ounces) shelled nuts
• shelled		4 ounces	• 1 cup nut halves or chopped nuts
• ground		4 ounces	• 1 cup, lightly packed

FOOD FAQs QUICK ANSWER

As a general rule, you can expect to get 1½-2 cups of nutmeat from 1 pound of nuts in their shells.

YIELDS & EQUIVALENTS

	BEFORE Preparation		AFTER Preparation
	Volume	**Weight**	**Approximate Yield**

ITALIAN-STYLE PASTA
MACARONI (dried, egg-free pasta)

- **rods and ribbons (thin or flat)**
  (i.e., angel hair, bavette, bucatini, cappellini, fideo, lasagna, linguine, spaghetti, tagliarini, vermicelli)

rods and ribbons	bundle 1" in diameter	2 ounces	• 1 cup cooked

- **shapes (e.g., bowties, farfalle, fusilli, gnocchi, rotelle, rotini, shells)**

	Volume	Weight	Approximate Yield
· large	$^3/_4$ cup	2 ounces	• $^5/_6$ - 1 cup cooked
· small	$^1/_2$ cup	2 ounces	• $^5/_6$ cup cooked

- **salad pasta (e.g., orzo, pastina, riso, salad macaroni, stellini)**

salad pasta	$^1/_4$-$^1/_2$ cup	2 ounces	• $^2/_3$-$^5/_6$ cup cooked

- **tubes (e.g., elbow, mostaccioli, penne, rigatoni, ziti)**

	Volume	Weight	Approximate Yield
· large	$^2/_3$-$^3/_4$ cup	2 ounces	• 1 cup cooked
· small	$^1/_2$ cup	2 ounces	• $^7/_8$ - 1 cup cooked

	BEFORE Preparation Volume	Weight	AFTER Preparation Approximate Yield
NOODLES (dried pasta with eggs)			
• regular or medium size	2 cups	3 ounces	• 1½ cups cooked
• extra wide (jumbo)	1½ cups	2 ounces	• 1 cup cooked
• extra wide yolkless	1¾ cups	2 ounces	• 1⅓ cups cooked
ORIENTAL NOODLES			
• bean thread (mung bean vermicelli)		1½ ounces	• 1⅓ cups (5 ounces) soaked
• rice sticks (maifun, rice vermicelli)		2 ounces	• 1 cup (5 ounces) soaked
• soba		2 ounces	• 1 cup (5 ounces) cooked
• somen		2 ounces	• 1 cup (8 ounces) cooked
• udon		2 ounces	• 1 cup (5 ounces) cooked

FOOD FAQs QUICK ANSWER

As a general rule, you can expect to get 6-9 cups of cooked pasta or noodles from 1 pound of dried product. The freshness of the product and the altitude at which it is cooked are among the factors that will affect your outcome.

YIELDS & EQUIVALENTS

	BEFORE Preparation		AFTER Preparation
	Volume	**Weight**	**Approximate Yield**
CHOCOLATE			
• chips or pieces	1 package	6 ounces	• 1 cup
• cooking bars or squares		1 ounce	• 1 tablespoon melted; *or* 4 tablespoons grated
COCOA POWDER	1/3 cup	1 ounce	• 4 cups cocoa
CORN SYRUP	12 fluid ounces	14 ounces	• 1½ cups
HONEY	1⅓ cups	1 pound	
MAPLE SYRUP	12 fluid ounces	14 ounces	• 1½ cups
MOLASSES	12 fluid ounces	18 ounces	• 1½ cups
SUGAR			
• brown (dark and light)	1 cup 3 cups	5⅓ ounces 1 pound	• ¾ cup firmly packed • 2¼ cups firmly packed
• granulated, brown	3¾ cups	1 pound	
• granulated, white	2 cups	1 pound	
• powdered (confectioners')	4 cups unsifted	1 pound	• 4½ cups sifted
• white, superfine	2¼- 2½ cups	1 pound	

	BEFORE Preparation		AFTER Preparation
	Volume	**Weight**	**Approximate Yield**
SUGAR CUBES	100-130 cubes	I pound	

SYRUP — See **CORN SYRUP** and **MAPLE SYRUP**.

Vegetables

	BEFORE Preparation		AFTER Preparation
	Volume	Weight	Approximate Yield
ARTICHOKE (globe)	I can	14 ounces	• 5 artichokes • 1½ cups, drained artichokes or pieces
ARUGULA (rocket) — See **GREENS, SALAD (spicy)**.			
ASPARAGUS	Spears: 12-15 extra large; 15-20 large; 21-27 medium; *or* 27-35 thin	I pound	• 2½-3 cups trimmed and cut into 1" pieces
AVOCADO — See **Fruits** section.			
BAMBOO SHOOTS	I whole (fresh or canned) I can	 8 ounces	• ¼-⅓ cup chopped • I cup drained, sliced or diced
BASIL — See **Herbs and Spices** section.			

	BEFORE Preparation		AFTER Preparation
	Volume	**Weight**	**Approximate Yield**
BEANS, dried			
• must be soaked (e.g., black, black-eyed pea, black turtle, cranberry, fava, flageolet, garbanzo, great Northern, kidney, lima, mung, navy, pink, pinto, red, soybeans, white beans)	I cup	6½-8 ounces	• 2½-3 cups soaked and cooked
• no soaking required (e.g., field peas, lentils, split peas)	I cup	7-8 ounces	• 2½-3 cups cooked

FOOD FAQs QUICK ANSWER

One pound of dried beans will yield 5-7 cups of soaked and cooked beans.
A 15-ounce can of beans will yield approximately 1½-1¾ cups of drained beans.

YIELDS & EQUIVALENTS

	BEFORE Preparation Volume	Weight	AFTER Preparation Approximate Yield
BEANS, edible pod			
• **Chinese long beans**	18 beans (15-18" long)	8 ounces	• 2-2¼ cups cut into 1" pieces
• **snap beans** (e.g., green, haricots vert, wax beans)	4 cups	1 pound	• 14 ounces trimmed beans; *or* 3 cups beans cut into 1" pieces
BEANS, fresh-shelled (e.g., cranberry, fava, lima beans)	4 cups in pod	1 pound in pod	• 1-1¼ cups shelled

FOOD FAQs QUICK ANSWER

When using frozen beans, a 9-ounce package will yield approximately 2 cups of thawed beans.

	BEFORE Preparation		AFTER Preparation
	Volume	Weight	Approximate Yield
BEETS — See also GREENS, TANGY (bitter).			
	4 medium without tops	I pound	• 2½-3 cups coarsely grated; or 3 cups diced
BELGIAN ENDIVE — See GREENS, SALAD (spicy).			
BROCCOLI	I average bunch	I¼ pounds	• 3-3½ cups raw small florets; or 5½-6 cups raw stems and florets
BRUSSELS SPROUTS		I pound	• 4 cups whole sprouts
CABBAGE			
• **head cabbage**	I average head	I½ pounds	• 6-8 cups shredded raw; or 3-4 cups shredded and cooked
• **Nappa cabbage**	I medium head	I¼-I½ pounds	• 8 cups shredded raw
CAPERS	I bottle	4 ounces	• 5 tablespoons, drained
CARROTS			
• **without tops**	I medium	3-4 ounces	• ½ cup diced, sliced or shredded
	2-3 large or 5-6 medium or 6-8 small	I pound	• 3 cups chopped, diced or sliced; or 2½ cups shredded
• **baby carrots**	25-30	12 ounces	• 2½ cups thinly sliced on diagonal

YIELDS & EQUIVALENTS

	BEFORE Preparation		AFTER Preparation
	Volume	Weight	Approximate Yield
CAULIFLOWER	I average head	I½-2 pounds	• 4½-5½ cups florets; or 2½-3 cups cooked
CELERY	3 medium stalks	5-7 ounces	• 1-1½ cups thinly sliced, chopped or diced
	I medium bunch	I½ pounds	• 3½-4 cups sliced, chopped or diced
CELERY ROOT (celeriac)	I root	I pound	• 2 cups diced or chopped; or 2½ cups julienne strips
CHICORY (curly endive) — See **GREENS, SALAD (spicy)**.			
CHILI PEPPER			
• fresh	depends on variety	I ounce	• 2 tablespoons chopped or sliced
• dried	depends on variety	I ounce	• 3 tablespoons crumbled or flaked
CHILIS, canned	I can	4 ounces	• ½ cup
CHIVES	I average bunch	I ounce	• 2 tablespoons snipped chives
CILANTRO — See **Herbs and Spices** section.			
COLLARD GREENS — See **GREENS, TANGY (bitter)**.			
CORN	2 ears	I½-1¾ pounds	• I cup kernels

	BEFORE Preparation Volume	Weight	AFTER Preparation Approximate Yield
CUCUMBER			
• field grown	1 medium	8-10 ounces	• 1½-2 cups chopped, sliced, diced or grated; *or* ¾-1 cup grated and squeezed dry
• hothouse (also known as greenhouse, burpless, English or European)	1 medium	12 ounces	• 2-2½ cups chopped, sliced, diced or grated; *or* 1-1¼ cups grated, squeezed dry
EGGPLANT			
• Italian or purple	1 medium	1 pound	• 5½-6 cups chopped or diced; *or* 1 cup cooked pulp
• Japanese	1 medium	5-6 ounces	• 1½-2 cups sliced or diced
• Chinese	1 medium	2½-3 ounces	• ¾-1 cup sliced or diced

ENDIVE — See **GREENS, SALAD (spicy)**.

ESCAROLE — See **GREENS, SALAD (spicy)**.

FENNEL — See **Herbs and Spices** section for **FENNEL LEAF**.

| | 1 medium bulb | 8 ounces | • 1⅓ cups sliced or diced |

YIELDS & EQUIVALENTS

	BEFORE Preparation Volume	Weight	AFTER Preparation Approximate Yield
GARLIC	I large head	2 ounces	• 10-15 cloves; *or* 6 tablespoons minced or chopped
		I large clove	• I teaspoon minced or chopped
		I medium clove	• ¾ teaspoon minced or chopped
		I small clove	• ½ teaspoon minced or chopped
GINGERROOT	I" slice of I½" diameter root	I ounce	• 2 tablespoons minced, shredded or grated, firmly packed

GREEN ONION — See **ONION, GREEN.**

FOOD FAQs QUICK ANSWER

To get ½ cup of vegetable purée, use 4 ounces of fresh vegetable *or* 1 cup of cooked and drained vegetable.

| | BEFORE Preparation | | AFTER Preparation |
	Volume	Weight	Approximate Yield
GREENS, SALAD (mild)			
• **lettuce**			
· **butterhead**	I medium head	12 ounces	• 8-10 cups torn leaves, loosely packed
· **iceberg**	I medium head	18 ounces	• 8-10 cups torn leaves, loosely packed
· **leaf lettuce**	I medium head	9 ounces	• 8-10 cups torn leaves, loosely packed
· **romaine**	I medium head	16 ounces	• 8-10 cups torn leaves, loosely packed
GREENS, SALAD (spicy)			
• **arugula (rocket)**	I bunch	4 ounces	• 4-5 cups tender stems and torn leaves, loosely packed
• **endive**			
· **Belgian**	I 4-6" long	3-4 ounces	• 8-12 leaves
· **curly (chicory)**	I medium head	¾-I pound	• 8-10 cups torn leaves, loosely packed
· **escarole**	I medium head	8-14 ounces	• 7-10 cups torn leaves, loosely packed
• **radicchio**	I head	9-10 ounces	• 7 cups leaves, torn and loosely packed
• **watercress**	I bunch	4-5 ounces	• 2-3 cups tender stems and torn leaves, loosely packed

YIELDS & EQUIVALENTS

	BEFORE Preparation Volume	Weight	AFTER Preparation Approximate Yield
GREENS, TANGY (bitter)			
• beet	I average bunch	I pound	• 6-8 cups leaves, torn and loosely packed
• collard	I average bunch	I pound	• 8 cups leaves, stems and ribs trimmed, loosely packed
• mustard	I average bunch	I2 ounces	• I3-I4 cups leaves, torn and loosely packed
• turnip	I average bunch	I pound	• I0-I2 cups trimmed leaves, loosely packed

FOOD
FAQs
QUICK
ANSWER

An average bunch of greens will cook down to approximately 1½ cups.

YIELDS & EQUIVALENTS

| | BEFORE Preparation | | AFTER Preparation |
	Volume	Weight	Approximate Yield
GREENS, TANGY (sharp)			
• kale	I average bunch	I2 ounces	• 10-12 cups trimmed leaves, loosely packed
• **spinach, fresh**	I average bunch	I pound	• 12 cups leaves, torn and loosely packed; or 1½-2 cups cooked and drained, coarsely chopped
	I package	10 ounces	• 12 cups leaves, torn and loosely packed
• **spinach, frozen**	I package	10 ounces	• 1¼ cups cooked; or I cup cooked and well drained
• **Swiss chard**	I average bunch	I pound	• 8 ounces stems & ribs; 8 ounces leaves • 10 cups torn leaves, loosely packed; or 2 cups sliced ribs and stems
HORSERADISH	I tapered root, 6-8" long, 2-2½" diameter	½ pound	• 1½ cups grated
JERUSALEM ARTICHOKE		I pound	• 2-2½ cups peeled, sliced or chopped
JICAMA	I average	I2 ounces	• 2½ cups peeled, cut into thin sticks or cubed
KALE — See **GREENS, TANGY (sharp)**.			

Vegetables

	BEFORE Preparation Volume	Weight	AFTER Preparation Approximate Yield
KOHLRABI	1 root	8-ounce bulb (12 ounces with stems and leaves)	• 1½-1⅔ cups julienne strips or diced
LEEK	1 medium	¾ pound, untrimmed	• ¾ cup sliced, white only; or 1¾ cups sliced, white and light green
LETTUCE — See **GREENS, SALAD (mild).**			
MUSHROOMS • **fresh** · **button**	4-6 medium 25-30 medium	3 ounces 1 pound	• 1 cup sliced • 5-6 cups sliced; or 2 cups sliced and cooked
· **wild**	depends on variety	3 ounces	• 1 cup sliced
• **canned**	1 can	4 ounces	• ⅔ cup drained, sliced or chopped
• **dried**	depends on variety	1 ounce	• 4-5 ounces rehydrated; or ⅔-1 cup rehydrated, drained and sliced
OKRA	2½ cups whole	8 ounces	• 2 cups sliced okra

	BEFORE Preparation Volume	Weight	AFTER Preparation Approximate Yield
ONION	I small	2-4 ounces	• ¼-½ cup chopped, diced or sliced
	I medium	4-7 ounces	• ½-I cup chopped, diced or sliced
	I large	7-9 ounces	• I-I½ cups chopped, diced or sliced
ONION, GREEN	I medium		• 2-3 tablespoons chopped or sliced, with green top
	I average bunch	4 ounces	• ⅓-½ cup sliced thin or in I" lengths, white & light green; *or*
			5-6 teaspoons sliced thin, white only

A 9-10 ounce package of most frozen vegetables provides approximately 2 cups of vegetables when thawed.

A 1-pound can of vegetables will provide approximately 2 cups of drained vegetables.

YIELDS & EQUIVALENTS

	BEFORE Preparation Volume	Weight	AFTER Preparation Approximate Yield
PARSLEY — See **Herbs and Spices** section.			
PARSNIP	4 medium	I pound	• 3 cups peeled and chopped, sliced or diced
PEAS, edible pod (e.g., sugar peas, sugar snap peas)	4 cups	I pound	• 4 cups whole or trimmed to I" lengths
PEAS, shell (e.g., English, fresh, garden peas)	4 cups in pod	I pound in pod	• I cup shelled peas
PEPPER, SWEET (bell) (green, red, yellow, etc.)	I medium	6-7 ounces	• 1-1½ cups thinly sliced; cut into ½" squares; or chopped
PIMENTO	I jar	4 ounces	• 5 tablespoons sliced
POTATO		I pound	• 2½-3 cups raw cut into I" cubes; or 1¾-2 cups cooked and mashed
• **round white**	3-4 potatoes		
• **red**	4-8 potatoes		
• **long white**	3-5 potatoes		
• **new (small)**	10-12 potatoes		
• **sweet**	2-3 potatoes		
• **Russet, Idaho**	2-3 potatoes		

	BEFORE Preparation		AFTER Preparation
	Volume	**Weight**	**Approximate Yield**
PUMPKIN — See **Fruits** section.			
RADICCHIO — See **GREENS, SALAD (spicy).**			
RADISH			
• **globe**	4 medium *or* 3 large, trimmed	2½ ounces	• ½ cup sliced
• **daikon**	1 (1-1½" diameter)	14 ounces	• 2-2½ cups sliced; *or* 2 cups shredded
ROCKET (arugula) — See **GREENS, SALAD (spicy).**			
RUTABAGA	1 medium	1 pound	• 3 cups diced; *or* 4 cups julienne strips
SALSIFY	8-10" root	2-3 ounces	• ⅓-½ cup sliced or diced
SHALLOT	1 medium head	1½-2 ounces	• 2-3 tablespoons diced or minced
SPINACH — See **GREENS, TANGY (sharp).**			
SQUASH, SPAGHETTI	1 medium	4-5 pounds	• 6 cups cooked flesh

YIELDS & EQUIVALENTS

	BEFORE Preparation Volume	Weight	AFTER Preparation Approximate Yield
SQUASH, SUMMER (e.g., chayote, crookneck, pattypan, straightneck, yellow squash, zucchini)	depends on variety	1 pound	• 3-3½ cups diced or sliced; or 2½ cups shredded
SQUASH, WINTER (e.g., acorn, buttercup, butternut, golden nugget, Hubbard)	depends on variety	1 pound	• 2 cups cooked pieces; or 1 cup cooked and mashed
SWISS CHARD — See **GREENS, TANGY (sharp)**.			
TOMATILLO	4 medium	6 ounces	• 1 cup finely chopped

TOMATO
  • **fresh**
	3 medium globe or
	8 small plum or
	25-30 cherry
		1 pound	• **Peeled and seeded:**
			  1½-2 cups chopped
			  Not peeled or seeded:
			  3 cups cut into ½" cubes; or
			  1-1¼ cups stewed and puréed

• **canned**	1 can	14½-16 ounce	• 1½ cups chopped or diced with juice; or 1 cup drained and chopped
• **sun-dried**	10-15 halves	1 ounce	• 3-4 tablespoons soaked and chopped

	BEFORE Preparation		AFTER Preparation
	Volume	**Weight**	**Approximate Yield**
TURNIP — See also **GREENS, TANGY (bitter).**			
	2 large *or* 3 medium (2-3" diameter)	I pound	• 3 cups sliced, diced or shredded
WATER CHESTNUT	I can	5 ounces	• I cup whole or sliced, drained
WATERCRESS — See **GREENS, SALAD (spicy).**			
ZUCCHINI	4-8 small *or* 3-4 medium	I pound	• 3-3½ cups diced or sliced; *or* 2 cups shredded and squeezed dry

	BEFORE Preparation		AFTER Preparation
	Volume	**Weight**	**Approximate Yield**
ALCOHOLIC BEVERAGES			
• beer	12-ounce can		• 1½ cups
• liquor/liqueur	1 fifth		• 17 jiggers (1½ ounces each)
• wine	750 ml bottle		• about 3⅕ cups
BAKING POWDER	1 cup	5½ ounces	
BROTH			
• bouillon cube	1 cube		• 1 cup when dissolved in 1 cup boiling water
• bouillon granules	1 teaspoon *or* 1 envelope		• 1 cup when dissolved in 1 cup boiling water
• canned	1 can	14½ ounces	• 1¾ cups
CATSUP — See **KETCHUP**.			
COFFEE			
• beans			
· light roast	2½ cups	½ pound	• 2½ cups ground; *or* 40 cups brewed coffee
· dark roast	3 cups	½ pound	• 3 cups ground; *or* 48 cups brewed coffee
• instant	1 cup powder	2 ounces	• 20 cups brewed coffee

	BEFORE Preparation Volume	Weight	AFTER Preparation Approximate Yield
GELATIN, unflavored	I envelope	¼ ounce	• I tablespoon powder
JUICE, FRUIT	I can	11½ ounces	• 1½ cups juice
• **frozen concentrate**	I can	12 ounces	• 1½ cups concentrate; *or* 48 ounces reconstituted (6 cups)
KETCHUP		16 ounces	• 1²/₃ cups
MARSHMALLOWS	8 regular	2 ounces	• I cup whole or snipped
	16 regular	4 ounces	• I cup melted
	100 miniature	2 ounces	• I cup whole
MAYONNAISE	I jar	32 ounces	• 4 cups
MUSTARD, prepared — See also **Herbs and Spices** section for **MUSTARD SEED**.			
	I jar	8 ounces	• 15 tablespoons (I cup minus I tablespoon)

Miscellaneous

Miscellaneous

	BEFORE Preparation		AFTER Preparation
	Volume	**Weight**	**Approximate Yield**
OLIVES			
• black			
· small with pits	14-16 olives	2 ounces	• ¼ cup pitted and chopped or sliced
· small without pits	20 olives	2 ounces	• ⅓ cup chopped or sliced
· medium without pits	17-19 olives	2 ounces	• ⅓ cup sliced or chopped
• green			
· small without pits	22 olives	2 ounces	• ⅓ cup sliced or chopped
· large with pits	5-6 olives	2 ounces	• ¼ cup pitted and chopped or sliced
· large without pits	10-12 olives	2 ounces	• ½ cup chopped or sliced
PEANUT BUTTER	I jar	8 ounces	• I cup
SALT			
• coarse or kosher	2 tablespoons	I ounce	
• table	I ½ tablespoons	I ounce	
	2 cups	I pound	
TOFU (bean curd)	I cake	12-14 ounces	• 2 cups in ¼" cubes; *or* 2 cups crumbled or mashed; *or* 1¾ puréed

	BEFORE Preparation		AFTER Preparation
	Volume	Weight	Approximate Yield
TOMATO PASTE	1 can	6 ounces	• 12 tablespoons (¾ cup)
TOMATO SAUCE	1 can	15 ounces	• 1⅔ cups
VINEGAR	12 fluid ounce bottle		• 1½ cups
WATER	1 tablespoon 2 cups	½ ounce 1 pound	
WHIPPED TOPPING • frozen • mix	 1 container 1 package	 8 ounces 4 ounces	 • 3½ cups • 2 cups whipped
YEAST (active dry)	1 package	¼ ounce	• 1 tablespoon

Index

Substitutions   **Yields & Equivalents**

	Substitutions	Yields & Equivalents

	Substitutions	Yields & Equivalents

	Substitutions	Yields & Equivalents

	Substitutions	Yields & Equivalents
Bowties (pasta)	............................in **PASTA, shapes** 84	....................in **MACARONI, shapes** 150
Bran, oat	See **OATS, bran** 78	 131
Bran, wheat	See **WHEAT** 107	 134
Brandy	............................in **LIQUOR** 66	..........See **ALCOHOLIC BEVERAGES** 170
Brazil nuts	 22	 147
	See also **NUTS** 77	See also *FOOD FAQs* **QUICK ANSWER** 149
Bread	............................See **BREADCRUMBS** 23	 129
	See also *FOOD FAQs* **QUICK ANSWER** 39	
Bread flour	See **FLOUR** 54	 131
Breadcrumbs	 23	 129
	See also *FOOD FAQs* **QUICK ANSWER** 39	
Brinza (cheese)	............................in **CHEESE, soft** 30	............................See **CHEESE, soft** 114
Broccoli	 23	 157
	See also *FOOD FAQs* **QUICK ANSWER** 50	See also *FOOD FAQs* **QUICK ANSWER** 165
Broth (or stock)	 23	 170
Broth, canned	See **BROTH** 23	 170
Brown rice	............................in **RICE** 90	............................See **RICE, brown** 133
	See also *FOOD FAQs* **QUICK ANSWER** 91	
Brown sugar	............................See **SUGAR, BROWN** 98	............................See **SUGAR** 152
Brussels sprouts	 23	 157
	See also *FOOD FAQs* **QUICK ANSWER** 50	

	Substitutions		Yields & Equivalents

	Substitutions		Yields & Equivalents	

	Substitutions	Yields & Equivalents

Substitutions	Yields & Equivalents

	Substitutions	**Yields & Equivalents**

	Substitutions	Yields & Equivalents

	Substitutions	Yields & Equivalents

Substitutions	Yields & Equivalents

	Substitutions		Yields & Equivalents	

	Substitutions	Yields & Equivalents

	Substitutions	Yields & Equivalents

	Substitutions	Yields & Equivalents

	Substitutions		Yields & Equivalents	

Substitutions	Yields & Equivalents

	Substitutions	Yields & Equivalents

	Substitutions	Yields & Equivalents

	Substitutions	Yields & Equivalents

	Substitutions	Yields & Equivalents

	Substitutions	Yields & Equivalents

O

INDEX

	Substitutions	**Yields & Equivalents**
Opah	in **FISH, full flavor (firm)** 53	See *FOOD FAQs* **QUICK ANSWER** 143
Orange	See **FRUIT (to be cooked), citrus** 57	124
	See also **ORANGE JUICE** 80	
	and **ORANGE PEEL** 80-81	
Orange blossom water	80	
Orange-flavored liqueur	See **LIQUOR** 67	See **ALCOHOLIC BEVERAGES** 170
Orange juice	80	in **ORANGE** 124
Orange peel (rind)	80-81	in **ORANGE** 124
Orange roughy	in **FISH, mild flavor (delicate)** 51	See *FOOD FAQs* **QUICK ANSWER** 143
Orange zest	See **ORANGE PEEL** 80-81	in **ORANGE** 124
	See also **ZEST OF FRUIT** 110	
Oregano	81	139
Oreos	See **COOKIE CRUMBS** 38	130
	See also *FOOD FAQs* **QUICK ANSWER** 39	
Oriental eggplant	See **EGGPLANT** 48	159
Oriental noodles	See **NOODLES** 77	151
Orzo (pasta)	in **PASTA, salad** 84	in **MACARONI, salad pasta** 150
Ouzo	in liqueur, licorice-flavored in **LIQUOR** 67	See **ALCOHOLIC BEVERAGES** 170
Oyster sauce	82	
Oysters	82	in **SHELLFISH, mollusks** 145

	Substitutions		Yields & Equivalents

	Substitutions	Yields & Equivalents

Substitutions	Yields & Equivalents

	Substitutions	Yields & Equivalents
Ravioli	....in **PASTA, stuffed** 84	..........See *FOOD FAQs* **QUICK ANSWER** 151
Red cabbage	See **CABBAGE** 25	 157
Red beans	in **BEANS, dried**.............................. 20	 155
	See also *FOOD FAQs* **QUICK ANSWER** 21	See also *FOOD FAQs* **QUICK ANSWER** 155
Red pepper, sweet (bell) See **PEPPER, SWEET (bell)** 86		 166
Red pepper flakes, hot	 90	...................................in **PEPPER, hot dried** 139
Red pepper sauce	.........................See **HOT PEPPER SAUCE** 63	
Red potato		....in **POTATO** 166
Red snapper	.........in **FISH, mild flavor (medium firm)** 51	..................See **FISH, whole (roundfish)** 143
Red wine vinegar	See **VINEGAR**...106	 173
Rhubarb	 90	 128
Rice	 90	 133
	See also *FOOD FAQs* **QUICK ANSWER** 91	
Rice, wild	See **WILD RICE**...108	 134
Rice flour	 91	
Rice sticks	.............................See **NOODLES, Oriental** 77	.......................in **ORIENTAL NOODLES** 151
Rice vermicelli	.............................See **NOODLES, Oriental** 77	.......................in **ORIENTAL NOODLES** 151
Rice vinegar	See **VINEGAR**...106	 173
Rice wine	.................................See **WINE, rice** 108	..........See **ALCOHOLIC BEVERAGES** 170
Ricotta cheese	.........................See **CHEESE, RICOTTA** 31	...................................in **CHEESE, soft** 114
	and in **CHEESE, soft** 30	

	Substitutions		Yields & Equivalents	
Rigatoni (pasta)	........................in **PASTA, tubes**	84	................in **MACARONI, tubes**	150
Riso (pasta)	.... See **PASTA, salad**	84	................in **MACARONI, salad pasta**	150
Rocket (arugula)	in **GREENS, SALAD (spicy)**.............	60		161
Rockfish	........in **FISH, mild flavor (medium firm)**	51	.... See *FOOD FAQs* **QUICK ANSWER**	143
Rolled oats	See **OATS**...........................	78		131
Romaine	in **GREENS, SALAD (mild)**.............	60		161
Romano cheese	in **CHEESE, hard**........................	29		113
Roquefort cheese	in **CHEESE, semisoft**.................	29		113
Rose water	....	91		
Rosemary	....	92		139
Rotelle (pasta)	........................in **PASTA, shapes**	84	................in **MACARONI, shapes**	150
Rotini (pasta)	........................in **PASTA, shapes**	84	................in **MACARONI, shapes**	150
Rum	........................in **LIQUOR**	67	..........See **ALCOHOLIC BEVERAGES**	170
Russet potato	....		................See **POTATO**	166
Rutabaga	....	92		167
Rye	....	92		133
Rye flour	....	92	..........See **FLOUR**	131
Sablefish	..........in **FISH, full flavor (medium firm)**	53	........See **FISH, whole (roundfish)**	143
Saffron	....	93		

	Substitutions	Yields & Equivalents

Substitutions	Yields & Equivalents

	Substitutions	Yields & Equivalents

	Substitutions		Yields & Equivalents

	Substitutions	Yields & Equivalents

	Substitutions	Yields & Equivalents

| Substitutions | Yields & Equivalents |

	Substitutions	Yields & Equivalents

	Substitutions	Yields & Equivalents